Bleng
Pastor Ke

What Readers are Saying About
Living A Transformed Life

Pastor Kevin West's ministry is replete with revelation knowledge. Revelation knowledge is divine thought translated to the finite mind; a knowledge that confronts and exceeds conventional wisdom. So as you read his book, the revelatory words will stir you, energize you and motivate you beyond the mundane to the meaningful; a life worth living.

Chuck Lawrence
Senior Pastor
Christ Temple Church

Pastor Kevin West, in this easy to read volume, powerfully and practically presents the essence of God's mission in history, i. e., transformation! The love and the purpose of God are expressed when transformation is realized in your life, your family, your church, and in our contemporary culture. This metamorphosis (as seen in the caterpillar becoming a butterfly) pictures God's desire to bring a beauty and quality of life that is more glorious than anyone can imagine. This book will change your life and transform your world.

Jim Hodges
Founder and President
Federation of Ministers and
Churches, International

Pastor Kevin West is a gifted, insightful man of God with a unique anointing to see past the surface of an issue, deep into the heart of the thing. His grasp of the concepts of Kingdom living, radical grace and his love of people make him a treasure to the Body of Christ. I'm proud to say he's my pastor, my confidant and my friend.

Rod Davis
Founder and Director
Kingdom Business Network

LIVING A TRANSFORMED LIFE

KEVIN WEST

WITH J. F. EDWARDS

FIRST EDITION

ISBN: 9781936989386

Library of Congress Control Number: 2012931229

Published by
NewBookPublishing.com, a division of Reliance Media, Inc.
2395 Apopka Blvd., #200, Apopka, FL 32703
NewBookPublishing.com

Printed in the United States of America

DEDICATION

I would like to dedicate this book to my wonderful wife, Leesa, and to my precious children, Lauren, Lindsey, Lakyn, Kaiden, and granddaughter, Braylie. Also, a special thank you to my parents Paul and Pat West, and my sister and brother-n-law Karen and Rob Arthur.

Contents

Acknowledgments.. 7

Introduction 9

PART I

What Did Jesus Mean?

Meeting a Mysterious Stranger Named Don 15

1   It's Here, It's Now.. 23

2   Mind-set Matters.. 35

3   God Wants You to Live in Victory.. 45

PART II

Who Am I Really?

Discovering Don's Past 59

4   Understand You Are a Child in God's Family............................ 65

5   God Inspires and Initiates 75

PART III

What Do I Choose?

Watching Don Change... 89

6   Growing Up and Maturing Is a Personal Choice 95

7   Select Friends Wisely 109

CONTENTS, *continued*

PART IV

WHAT IS MY PURPOSE?

Watching Me Change 121

8   Know that You Are Given Authority...........................127

9   Change Happens...137

10   Know the Purpose of God's Anointing Upon Your Life......153

Hearing from My Friend...159

Selected Scripture References...*161*

About the Author..*207*

Acknowledgments

The crafting of this book has been a five-year journey in the making. I originally began writing this book in July 2006; however, all the pieces didn't come together until March 2011.

I want to especially thank my precious wife, Leesa, for her love and steadfastness. She, along with our daughters, Lauren, Lindsey, Lakyn, and son, Kaiden, have stood with me, sacrificed, and sown me into the ministry.

I wish to thank my parents, Paul and Pat West, and my sister and brother-in-law, Karen and Robin Arthur, for their loving support and encouragement.

I am thankful to Pastor Chuck and Jamie Lawrence for their dedication to our Lord and for embracing my family when we first came to Christ Temple Church.

A special thanks to J.F. Edwards for helping me capture the essence of the revelation and story line.

INTRODUCTION

Jesus said something very curious when He first began his ministry. After being tempted in the wilderness and then entering Capernaum, He said, "The kingdom of heaven is at hand" (Matt. 4:17). From that point in time until His crucifixion, He said this over and over.

When the people of Capernaum experienced numerous healings and begged Jesus to stay, He told them He had to "preach the kingdom of God to other cities also" (Luke 4:42-44).

He spent many hours conveying the kingdom to people through parables. He compared it to a man sowing good seed in the ground (Matt. 13:24-30). He said the kingdom was like the tiny mustard seed growing large enough to house birds in her branches (Matt. 13:31-32). He also referred to it as being like leaven in bread (Matt. 13:33).

The kingdom of God is mentioned more than a hundred times in the New Testament and it is the central theme of Jesus' messages recorded in the gospels. What was Christ trying to tell us? Why did He teach more on this subject than even the cross?

Clearly, the Lord didn't come to earth only to purchase our salvation. His purpose extended far beyond this. God became man to live among us to initiate something greater than our finite minds can comprehend.

Jesus came to restore our relationship with Him and reestablish our dominion on this earth He had given to Adam. This is more than cleansing our sins. It is the returning to each of us all that we are meant to be. From here begins our intimate journey with Christ. This is what God planned long before He spoke the earth and stars and all that is living into existence. As we understand this truth we will not only experience the abundant life but also look with greater anticipation "for that blessed hope, and the glorious appearing of the great God and our Saviour Jesus Christ" (Titus 2:13).

Every Christian desires a meaningful and victorious life. We want to experience what we read in Psalm 1, where it describes the way the Lord intimately knows the way of the righteous and prospers all his pursuits. Moreover, at the end of our life we want to hear Jesus say we were good and faithful servants. Yet, few of us ever understand how to obtain this. We flounder about, unfaithful to our calling and never find contentment.

For some years now I have asked the Lord to show me what it would mean to live in the kingdom of heaven. After all, Jesus said that it was in our midst, and yet most people feel defeated, never living out all that Jesus said was possible. This book represents what God gave me in answer to my prayer. I pray now that God will enlighten this generation to all that He means by the kingdom of heaven being at hand. Then we will understand why Jesus compared the kingdom to a treasure hidden in a field. In this parable, when a man first discovers the treasure, he joyfully sells all that he owns so that he may obtain it (Matt. 13:44).

PART I

WHAT DID JESUS MEAN?

Meeting a Mysterious Stranger Named Don

Late one night in January 1997, I was still working at my computer when I was startled by my wife, Leesa, standing in the doorway. With one arm around our oldest daughter and holding our youngest girl on her hip, she stood silently studying me. I could tell she was upset.

"What is it? I asked.

"We just came down to give you a good night kiss."

I waited for her to bring the girls closer but she didn't move.

"We don't even know who you are anymore," she said. She then turned and left the room with our daughters.

Her words cut right through me. I stood and started to follow after her but stopped myself. What could I say to her? I knew she was right. She didn't know who I was because I didn't even know.

I was in deep trouble, and she had no idea. I had drifted far from my faith. My pursuit of success had driven me to illegal practices at the bank where I was vice president. I was now facing the possibility of getting caught and going to prison. I didn't know what I was going to do.

I sat back down at my computer and tried to work but couldn't. The truth of my wife's words forced me to examine myself.

I began pacing back and forth from my office to the living room, agonizing over my predicament. I was cornered with absolutely no chance of escape. I felt as if I were suffocating. I had no friend or family member who could help me.

At one point I stood at our bay window to watch the onset of a rainstorm. Harsh winds bent thin saplings almost to the ground and snapped the rotten limbs of some of the older trees. It was as if God were washing everything clean as an example for me. I looked out for a long time, staring at the rain beating against the window, reflecting upon my life.

My mother had raised me to love the Lord. She didn't just talk about following Christ, but lived it. Somehow she always found out about families in need and bought extra groceries for them. Early on Saturday mornings while my friends watched cartoons in their pajamas, my father would drive me to a home designated by my mother, and I would secretly leave a bag of food on the doorstep.

I just couldn't bear the thought of telling such a good mother as this about my wrongdoing. Worst of all, however, was having to tell Leesa. She exemplified all that was tender and right in a wife. She was the virtuous woman described in Proverbs 31 whose children rise up and call her blessed, and whose husband safely trusts in her. I deeply loved her and my children and knew they deserved much better than what I had become.

That night I remembered my mother once saying to me, "when your back is up against the wall, don't run *from* God but run *to* Him."

· At 1:30 in the morning, having paced and cried for three hours, I called out to God. "Lord," I prayed, "If you'll just take this mess from me, then I'll give it to you."

I can't describe exactly what happened at that moment, except to say I was suddenly released from my burden. I knew I had to face the consequences of my wrong, but now I was safely held in the palm of my Father's hand. The weight had lifted.

I sat back down at my computer and typed out my resignation to the bank.

The next day after I came home I held Leesa and told her everything. At first she could hardly believe it. When she finally broke into tears, I knew the immensity of her pain was because of her love for me. We both agreed that I had to walk in truth and then face whatever the consequences with no attempt to conceal anything.

I had purchased a small corner grocery store just two years earlier as an investment and began managing it in March as a means of income. I figured this way I could pay our bills as I waited for what was ultimately coming with the civil suit and the indictment.

The store was small with only four aisles and a deli, but I was overwhelmed by it. I didn't know anything about ordering stock or pricing items or even operating the cash register. I was struck with how my indiscretion had so quickly moved me from my position as vice president of a bank to a storekeeper cutting meat for sandwiches. However, I wasn't the same person anymore. Chasing after success was no longer my priority. I now hungered to really know this Christ to whom I had committed myself. Instead of thinking of what people could give me, I wanted to know how I could help them. I no longer wanted selfishness, but selflessness, to characterize my life.

Giving freely to others was a new direction, but I didn't know how to practice good judgment. I began giving credit to anyone who came into my store and asked for it. After they filled out a simple application they could walk out with a bag of groceries. It wasn't long before word spread and my number of patrons increased. Most people paid me back, but a few left with free food, and I never saw them again.

People of every age and economic stratum passed through the store. Local business people dropped in to grab a drink or snack. Young unwed mothers came for free milk for their babies. Elderly people from a nearby high-rise sometimes needed a few staples until they received their social security check. The neighborhood children came in frequently for candy, and a number of people wandered in with obvious addiction problems.

This seemingly insignificant business gave me the opportunity to interact with hundreds of people and share my testimony. Over time I had befriended a number of customers who came in regularly, sometimes lingering at my counter just to share their problems with me. Between customers, I would read the Scriptures and listen to sermons on the TV across from my counter. I also rewrote each of the epistles in a notebook, paraphrasing each passage so I could understand their meaning.

On a bright morning in May I heard the buzzer at the front door and looked up from my Bible. An old man with a long unkempt beard paused in the entrance and scanned the store. He was dressed in a soiled shirt and tattered trousers. When he saw me, he smiled and moved slowly toward the counter with a limp.

"How are you?" he asked.

"Fine," I said.

"Can I get a little credit?"

"Sure," I answered.

The man's gray hair was greasy and combed back off his face, almost touching his shoulders. When he talked I noticed he had no teeth. His clothes smelled sour as he came closer and rested his hands on the counter. He didn't look healthy. He coughed and cleared his throat often. His heavy-framed glasses were slightly tinted and looked twenty years behind the times.

When he noticed I was reading the Bible, he asked, "Are you getting anything good out of that book?"

"It's *all* good," I said.

"Jesus," he said, "is revealed from cover to cover, from Genesis to Revelation."

I didn't know how he had concluded this, so I just sort of nodded.

"May I show you?" he asked.

I said, "Yes," and with the Bible still facing me he turned the pages back through the Old Testament. His hands were dirty and his nails untrimmed. He stopped in the third chapter of Genesis and ran his finger down the page, resting it on the phrase, "tree of life."

"This is Jesus," he said. "Most people believe that God placed the flaming sword at the Garden of Eden to keep man away, but this isn't true. The sword is the Word of God pointing the way to the tree of life."

He then flipped to Numbers where Moses made a brass serpent and raised it on a pole.

"The serpent represents Christ on the cross," he said. "Whenever the Israelites gazed upon it they were healed."

As he turned from book to book in the Bible all the way to Revelation, showing me passages portraying Christ, I was amazed. I had read these same Scriptures many times but had never seen what he was now pointing out.

He told me his name was Don and he appreciated me giving him groceries. I watched him fill out the credit application, not sure what to think of him.

After he picked out a few items he thanked me again. "I'll see you later," he said. Then he turned and left.

His application only mentioned the route number of his residence. No specific address was given.

I didn't know at the time that I was going to become friends with this broken man and we were going to spend almost every day together for the next two years until I entered prison. God had brought him to me to be my mentor. Our friendship and growth in Christ was going to initiate the establishment of the kingdom of heaven not only in my life but also in his.

"From that time Jesus began to preach, and to say, Repent: for the kingdom of heaven is at hand."

Matthew 4:17

Chapter One

It's Here, It's Now

The Abundant Life

Jesus said that He came not only to give us life but that we "might have it more abundantly" (John 10:10). So different is this life he offers, that 2 Corinthians 5:17 says those in Christ are completely new creatures. All which was part of a person before salvation is forever gone. Everything becomes new.

Why then are so many Christians miserable? They want this new life, but their Christian walk is oppressive and burdensome. They struggle and work harder rather than enjoy the freedom Jesus promises.

The problem is not their sincerity, for they truly want to obey God. In fact, the more they fail, the harder they try, promising the Lord over and over that they'll do better.

The problem is they haven't understood what Jesus was saying about the kingdom of heaven. Instead, they are living out religious routine which is empty of all life. This man-made religion may be a bunch of rules imposed by a church or it could be what someone creates for himself.

Many times we set standards for ourselves based on what we

think we should be, none of which are scriptural. Even more elusive is trying to fulfill the expectations of what we think others have of us. The result is internal conflict, in which we constantly try to gain a sense of security by pleasing others. We struggle in this same way in an attempt to please God.

Jesus offers us something much different, something liberating.

Seeing from God's Perspective

One of the earliest recorded instructions of Jesus found in the New Testament is "Repent, for the kingdom of heaven is at hand" (Matt. 4:17). One of the simplest explanations of the word "repent" is to see things from God's perspective. The demand for changing our understanding is because of the momentous time in history of Jesus bringing the kingdom of God to us. Once we allow the Lord to open our hearts to what this means, it will liberate and empower us.

Jesus preached this message to people who were oppressed by the Romans and living in physical bondage. They were bound by the rules of the Pharisees and their religious systems.

Living in a country free from government oppression and religious laws, however, doesn't negate the need for the liberating words of Christ. People can still be enslaved by financial debt, addictions, a craving for approval, or any number of strongholds.

Jesus' words spoken more than 2,000 years ago are still true for us today. His teachings are never bound or limited by time or place. He invites you and me to see the kingdom from His perspective, because he wants us to know the truth.

First, we must recognize that the kingdom of heaven is in our midst this very moment. Jesus came to earth to establish it with all His divine principles and blessings. Once we know Him, then we become a part of His great plan to liberate us from every fear and entanglement, from anything which inhibits us to experience an abundant life.

Some people grow up in a religious tradition which destroys hope for this life. They are convinced to just plod along, enduring their problems, with no expectation that God will, or even care, to intervene. Their only option, they feel, is to wait until eternity before they can experience freedom from their misery.

This perspective is no less tragic than the Jews looking past our Lord for another savior. Jesus was the real Messiah walking right in their midst, and yet some were so misguided they kept looking for His arrival in the future. In the same way, if we only see heaven as our celestial destination after our death, we miss God's grandest plan for us now in this life on Earth.

This incredible journey begins with throwing off our old perspective so we can embrace all Jesus has given us. He is saying, "It's here! Now! The kingdom of heaven is right here in front of your face."

An Analogy

Let's suppose you have inherited from your father a large estate including a picturesque mansion with a new car and clothes and money. This is good news because you are presently struggling financially. Paint is curling off your dilapidated house, your clothes are worn threadbare, and a rusty bicycle carries you back and forth to work. Then just before the inheritance is transferred to you, someone breaks into the mansion and steals the checkbook to your new account. The thief writes checks freely for whatever he desires. It's your money meant to bless you, but he uses it for himself. He ruins the beauty of your father's mansion, filling it with tasteless furniture and lamps and gaudy rugs. He wears the new suits which were hanging on a rack for you, and carelessly speeds around in your new car. Then he begins acting and talking like you. He mixes with your friends and spends time with your family, not only taking over your relationships, but ruining them. This thief wholly enjoys the influence and position that is rightfully yours.

At your greatest moment of despair, someone bigger and stronger than the thief comes to you and explains that you are still entitled to the complete inheritance. He says the thief is too powerful for you to fight, but not for him. He vows to crush him and to return everything back to you. Then he goes out, defeats and binds your enemy, and restores your inheritance. The money is back in the checking account, all the gaudy trappings purchased for the house are gone, and everything is returned new. The relationships with your family and friends are restored. In fact, they are even better than they were before everything had been stolen.

Jesus is the one who came and bound Satan, the thief. He is the one who has defeated the Enemy and restored our lives. This is why we call Him our Savior.

Garden of Eden

To fully understand the kingdom of God, we must begin

with the Garden of Eden. Here we see the order of God's plan. After He created the earth flourishing with plants and wildlife, He planted this garden and placed Adam there to tend to it. Adam was also given the authority to name every animal and bird God created (Genesis 2:8-20). He and Eve both enjoyed an intimate relationship with God, sitting in His presence, conversing with Him face-to-face.

Genesis 1:26 explains how God made mankind to oversee the fish, the birds, the cattle, and all that's in the earth. Adam and Eve were given the responsibility of being the first managers of what was heaven on earth.

Then Satan deceived them with the lie that they could live independently from God. When Adam and Eve sinned, their relationship with the Father was severed. They both felt the pangs of this separation even before they were told the consequences of their disobedience. They each felt alienated from the Lord for the first time in their lives. They experienced fear and shame, and tried to hide from God (Genesis 3:1-10).

Earth Created For Man

God reigns in heaven, but He created earth for man to rule. Psalms 115:16 says, "The heaven, even the heavens, are the Lord's: but the earth hath He given to the children of men." Adam and Eve were supposed to have dominion over all creation. Their mission was to establish the kingdom of heaven here on earth. Before their disobedience, they were intertwined with God through the Holy Spirit, knowing the Lord intimately and understanding His heavenly principles. God's Spirit gave them wisdom and the capability to carry out their mission. When they chose independence they became alienated from God and each other. They even became alienated from themselves and what they were supposed to be.

Jesus came to set everything back in order. He came to draw us into a love relationship with Him so that we may live out the kingdom of heaven now. When we say yes to Him, the Holy Spirit positions us within the kingdom of God. Everything that is in the heavenly places is available to us.

The earth has been created for us and our children and our children's children. When we come to know Jesus, we are in a vibrant relationship with God just as Adam and Eve were before their fall. God intends for us to reign over the earth through the power of the Holy Spirit. This authority involves much more than overseeing His wildlife and natural resources. It grants dominion over every entanglement and struggle.

Like Adam and Eve, we can choose independence from God and remain in darkness. We too can deceive ourselves into thinking there is a better way apart from His heavenly principles, but the result will be misery and defeat.

The Lord wants us to live free from every element of darkness. He wants our days filled with vision and victory. Only through Him is a new life possible.

Two Governments

There are millions of people not connected to the life-giving flood of mercy that Jesus brings. God's answer for them is right in their midst, but they do not receive it. They live outside the kingdom of heaven.

It is helpful to understand that two spiritual forces are at work. The government of darkness is void of God's leadership. In this case, Man is in charge and acting from a state of darkness which invariably leads to failure. In contrast, God's government, called the kingdom of heaven, operates from divine principles. The Lord is the ruler, releasing His power and wisdom to His people.

God's Plan

When Adam and Eve broke their relationship with God they lost dominion over their surroundings and themselves. Their circumstances, fleshly appetites, and the earth's elements now controlled them (Genesis 3:16-19). Therefore, they lacked everything they needed to reign over the earth.

Because of their rebellion, man is now subject to his daily trials. Instead of having dominion over the earth, the earth and all it's elements now have dominion over us.

However, our separation from God through sin does not change God's plan. He still wants to draw us into a relationship with Him and to establish His kingdom here on earth. Jesus, God in the flesh, came to us to declare that the kingdom of heaven is at hand. He has bound the thief and is here to return to us every spiritual blessing which was lost due to Adam's and Eve's rebellion.

The ministry of Jesus was more than miracles and healings. All these works were the outpouring of the kingdom of heaven. Every sign and wonder was a declaration of what God was bringing to pass. His plan to restore His relationship with mankind and to establish the kingdom of heaven on earth prompted the heavenly chorus of angels to praise God. They shouted, "Peace on Earth and good will toward men" (Luke 2:14).

Many ignore God's calling and seek substitutes to right themselves and escape their state of alienation. But it never works. Drugs, or alcohol, a religion of self, or any human pursuit cannot fulfill the deep needs of anyone. To these people, Jesus proclaims the kingdom of heaven is available right now for them.

We all must decide how we wish to live. We either stumble about blindly in darkness or we embrace the abundant life that Jesus is offering.

Two Religious Groups

In the day of Jesus, the Pharisees and the Sadducees were two dominant religious groups among the Jews. The Pharisees knew the Mosaic Law very well. They believed the prophets and anticipated the coming of the Messiah, but they never recognized Jesus as the One prophesied in their Scriptures. Instead, they were convinced He would come one day in the future. Unlike the Pharisees, the Sadducees did not believe in the resurrection. Paul clarifies a major difference between the two groups, saying, "For the Sadducees say that there is no resurrection, neither angel, nor spirit: but the Pharisees confess both" (Acts 23:8). Too many in the church today are influenced by a pharisaical spirit, agreeing God is able to do anything, far beyond what they can ask or even imagine, but they don't expect any change to happen now. It is easier for them to expect that better times will come or are coming in the future. They fail to recognize that the kingdom of heaven is already here. Instead of living in victory, they suffer in defeat.

Some Christians today could be compared to the Sadducees in that they don't recognize the resurrected life. They don't understand the power of Christ that has defeated not only sin and the grave but the darkness of this world. They deny themselves a life directed and empowered by the Holy Spirit because they don't believe it is possible.

Both kinds of Christians may be well-intentioned, but neither group experiences the abundant life. They may read the Bible, pray, and display what appears to be the model life of a saint, but they're missing out on God's greatest journey.

Dominion Reestablished

Jesus was willing to sacrifice everything so He could bring us back into a relationship with the Father. He knew he was facing humiliation, torture and death, but He only thought of us. Reestablishing our dominion and position required His death, burial, and resurrection. With the horrific ending of His life approaching, He calls His disciples with the tender term, "little flock," and tells them not to fear. He continues in Luke 12:32, explaining, "It is your Father's good pleasure to give you the kingdom."

Establishing the kingdom of God means more than simply attending church. Sadly, many churches neglect teaching about the kingdom, or they don't even know how to identify it. This is tragic because the meeting of believers should provide the gateway through which others understand restoration of our dominion. Instead, we sometimes gather on a Sunday as a place just to socialize.

We all must cultivate an imagination for the things of God. We need to think beyond our own limited views. Nicodemus could not understand when Jesus said, "Except a man be born of water and of the Spirit, he cannot enter into the kingdom of God" (John 3:5). He thought Christ was talking about a physical birth. Paul clarifies that the kingdom of God is far deeper than the physical realm, saying, it "is not meat and drink but righteousness, and peace, and joy in the Holy Ghost" (Rom. 14:17).

As our understanding deepens, we will not only sing about a better life in eternity but we will also experience dominion over circumstances and claim victory now. Jesus taught us to pray, "Thy kingdom come. Thy will be done in earth, as it is in heaven" (Matt. 6:10). His prayer makes it clear that God's government is to expand on earth through His people.

Establishing God's kingdom should be the outpouring of our worship. The life of a Christian is not to be oppressive. Jesus says His yoke is easy and His burden is light (Matt. 11:30). The reason living out God's purpose is freeing is because it is accomplished through the work of the Holy Spirit. No one is able to perform the works of God independently, for man-made rules and procedures only produce frustration.

Just a glimpse of the heavenly elements can make a difference. Seeing the kingdom of heaven in our midst right now, can change us, our families, our city, and affect change for the world.

This grand journey begins with asking Christ to forgive your sins and to fill you with His Holy Spirit. Trust Him to restore the fullness of your spiritual inheritance and establish the kingdom of heaven through you.

*"The heavens declare the glory of God;
and the firmament showeth his handiwork."*

Psalm 19:1

Chapter Two

Mind-set Matters

Your World View

Did you know that each of us has constructed a world view? We draw from our experiences, good and bad, building our unique perspective on life. How we perceive everything is determined in part by how we were raised. Some people are nurtured by two loving parents while others come from broken homes. Some people are born in wealth, while others only know generations of poverty. A background of education, church, and work, or the lack thereof, all contribute to shaping a person. Without even realizing it, brick by brick, we are continually building our world view.

What does going home for Christmas mean to you? Someone from a big city might reminisce about the bright holiday lights strung through a busy downtown. It might warm their heart thinking of crowds bustling from store to store with armfuls of packages. Christmas for another person might mean the quiet solitude of a tiny cabin set back in a snow-covered hollow. Whether someone grew up in the mountains of Tennessee or on the tropical islands of Hawaii, their interpretation of Christmas will differ. And yet, these varying images will produce for each of them a familiar sense of home.

Our view of God is shaped in the same way. How we grow up, how we are taught, even how people treat us- all will influence our perspective of God. For example, many times our view of our heavenly Father is determined by the relationship we have with our dad.

World Cultures

This conglomeration of mind-sets ends up sitting in the pews of every church. The church is then charged with communicating the Word of God in a way which cuts through any misconceptions and presents the truth accurately. This is a holy calling. The kingdom of God is to be planted and established all over the world, despite the differences in world views or theology.

The culture of our Father and His kingdom is the only true unifying force. His principles unite people from every country and from every walk of life.

Most of the time we try to force the Scriptures to fit our own perspective, rather than allowing God's word to shape us. After filtering the truths of God through our preconceived notions and beliefs, we distort the teachings of the Bible and ultimately do not experience the promises and blessings. God's living Word challenges the very core of what we believe and even how we think.

Refusing to abandon preconceived beliefs as we study the Bible is like refusing to discard the old sofa in our living room when bringing in a new one. We must abandon the way we once thought so that we can fully embrace what is new. Holding on to an old mind-set impedes the fullness of God's Word in our lives, and keeps us on our same old path of living.

Matthew 9:17 emphasizes this new life, saying, "Neither do men put new wine into old bottles: else the bottles break, and the wine runneth out, and the bottles perish: but they put new wine into new bottles, and both are preserved."

Authority of God's Word

The principle of "mind-set matters" points to the source of our growth: the Bible. Every thought and action must be aligned with God's Word. When we commit ourselves to the Scriptures, knowing they are the final authority, we will have a compass which will always point us in the right direction.

Jesus clarified in Luke 4:4 that food by itself is not enough to complete a person's life, that man must also live by "every word of God." The Bible is the only reliable source to enlighten us to the specifics about God and his kingdom.

As we meditate upon the Living Word, mulling it over in our minds, slowly turning it in our imaginations, the truths eventually became a part of us. We come into an understanding of His authority. This experience is more than simply reading about other people in the Bible. The Lord enlightens us on how to heal broken relationships, how to manage money, how to face tragedies, how to live day-to-day within His grace.

The more we align our lives with His Words, the more we prosper. In fact, Jesus says in John 14:12, "He that believeth on me, the works that I do shall he do also; and greater works than these shall he do; because I go unto my Father."

Jesus has authority from His Father, and then He imparts

authority to us. When we accept Him as our Savior, the Lord adopts us into the family of God as His child. He literally becomes our heavenly Father and watches over us with our best interests in mind.

Authority in the Church

Authority in the church is similar. Pastors are supposed to watch over their congregation with love and the protective feelings of a father. But this responsibility is not limited to only the pastor. There should be other mature believers in the body of Christ with the same heart to nurture others.

Nurturing believers is a deeper commitment than simply teaching them. Paul clarifies the difference in 1 Corinthians 4:15, saying, "For though ye have ten thousand instructors in Christ, yet have ye not many fathers: for in Christ Jesus I have begotten you through the gospel." He points out that while there is an abundance of teachers, there are few who will mentor a young believer. In the family of God, some are especially called to take on the role as parents.

Caring for the flock in this manner has nothing in common with manipulation, for love is at the heart of true spiritual authority in the church. Leaders and mentors are to nurture believers in the Word of God and then trust the Lord for the growth. They should have the mind-set of trusting and releasing the power of the Lord through His people.

Manipulating and controlling people to force growth are not God's ways. Touting rules and heaping guilt on people, all with the purpose of forcing them to follow the church's direction, represents more of a cult than an assembly of believers. It may appear successful for a season, but after a point the darkness of this approach will become apparent.

It is vital to find the right kind of spiritual parent, one who is a mature Christian with a heart for investing themselves into your life. Pray as you search. Then approach that person who displays the fruits of the Spirit, whose life reflects Christ, the kind of person you wish to emulate. A number of godly men and women will welcome the opportunity to invest into your life, if you only ask them. They want to release into other lives all God has imparted to them.

The desire of a mature Christian to mentor and shape another Christian is similar to the desire of a father wanting to nurture his own children. For example, I am dedicated to raising my children to become committed Christians, strong citizens, faithful spouses, and loving parents. My wife and I invest everything possible into raising them to become responsible adults. If we neglect our duty to teach them the truths of Scripture and how to live, then we are not good parents. If we encourage them to stay at home and live self-indulgent, indifferent lives, then we are forsaking our calling. The love we have for our children impels us to release into their lives all that God has imparted to us. Spiritual parents are given the same kind of responsibility for the church.

Unclogging the Flow

Everyone faces problems, such as losing a job, becoming sick, or facing the death of a loved one. The challenge to endure or find a new direction can only come from God. The glory hidden in every kind of trouble is the fact that God wants to help us. He wants to intervene. Psalm 121:2 declares that "help cometh from the Lord, which made heaven and earth."

Why in the face of trials do we not experience victory or receive comfort? Instead of experiencing the intervention of God, we struggle and hope we can just endure a little longer.

There is a reason why the Lord's power is inhibited in our lives, sometimes during the most tragic times. The problem is with us. We don't experience the turning of our situation because something in our lives is quenching the outpouring of His Spirit. It's as if an endless reservoir of water is rushing through a pipe to irrigate a field, but it's halted by a clogged filter. Once that filter is clean of all filth and debris, the water will gush out over the ground, nourishing the seed, and bringing forth life.

This filter is our minds. We don't think clearly because our minds do not align with the truth of the Scriptures. We live in darkness and fool ourselves into thinking that we are living in light. We are ignorant to the fact that we are blind. Until we allow God to change our mind-sets, we will continue receiving the same results of a struggling existence. Our limited experiences and narrow world view will stunt our spiritual growth. In Romans 12:2, Paul explains we are to transform our lives by renewing our minds. Our vision of life must be so in tune with God and His Word, we should live out His precepts and promises without effort or conscious thought.

Declaring His Glory

When David presents his song of thanksgiving in 1 Chronicles

16:24, he charges us to declare God's "glory among the heathen; His marvelous works among all nations." His psalm praises God's faithfulness and instructs us to remember His covenant. This exuberant song follows the celebration of the return of the Ark of God. After being stolen by the Philistines and held for several months, then residing for twenty years in Kirjathjearim, it is finally moved to Jerusalem (1Sam 5:1, 6:1-21, 7:1-2, 2 Sam 6:1-15). This is a personal celebration for Israel, but they are encouraged to declare God's great works to everyone, Jew and Gentile alike.

This passage conveys the influence we are to have on others. A life of victory and praise is a strong testimony for our faith. People may not always believe what we say, but they will always believe what we do. A transformed life speaks much louder than any sermon.

The word *declare* in the Hebrew means to keep score. With this in mind, we can think of our life as a scoreboard with people constantly watching the results. The number of spectators may differ for each of us depending on the size of our influence, but we are still being watched. Our lives are like the song of David, declaring through our actions all of our victories and praises for God.

Have you ever compared the lives of Christians and nonbelievers and saw no differences? Sadly, this is too often the case. What the world needs to see are victorious Christians who are living out the kingdom of God. This is how God expects His children to be effective kingdom builders.

People are watching us very closely at work, at school, at church, and everywhere else we go. They're watching how we treat our spouse, nurture our children, and handle adversity. Many are listening closely to our words and examining our actions. If they see that we have victory, especially in the midst of trouble, they will be drawn to this new life in Christ.

In addition to being watched by people on earth, Paul points out in Hebrews 12:1 we are also surrounded by the great crowd of saints who have passed on before us. This alone should encourage us to throw off every hindrance, as this verse says, and run the race ahead of us.

Our scoreboards need to look like runaway wins, with bright lights flashing high victories. We shouldn't be only running neck-to-neck with the world. Our lives should stand out. Our scorecard should tally much higher for people to take notice. We should lead lives which are way above and beyond what is usual.

Someone should be able to look at our lives and see there is something unusual about us which produces victory. People should be so bowled over by the way we live that they say, "Even when he gets down, he still comes out on top. Even when it doesn't look like it is going in his favor, he still bounces back."

This new life is possible if we allow God's Word to change our mind-sets and align our lives with His truths. In turn, this will bring us to the place where we recognize that we have authority over our circumstances and over our feelings. When we walk in the light of God's word and experience the fullness of His kingdom, our life will become a song of victory. This will be sweet music in God's ear and an inviting melody to those around us who are in desperate need of hope.

"Nay in all these things we are more than conquerors through him that loved us."

Romans 8:37

Chapter Three

GOD WANTS YOU
TO LIVE IN VICTORY

Living in Light

God wants our lives to be triumphant. He desires us to experience all He has promised. In turn, He wants each of our personal victories to become a testimony to His life-changing power. In this way, he draws the lost into the family of God.

People can see the glory of God through our lives in so many ways. We might write a letter of encouragement to someone who is hurting and the words minister to them in a divine way. The tenderness we display toward our wife and children demonstrates the love of Christ. Every time we conduct business honestly, we display God's principles. The Lord can take the smallest contribution of an obedient believer and bring enlightenment to someone who is watching.

When God created the world He first spoke light into being. After seeing it was good, He then separated it from darkness (Genesis 1:3-4). Therefore, light and dark can never co-exist. They are complete opposites. Darkness vanishes in a room once light is introduced.

It is no wonder that the Scriptures speak of obedience as walking in light and disobedience as being in darkness. These two lifestyles are entirely opposed to each other. When we are walking in the light, we are drawing upon Christ and experiencing the true fullness of who He is. On the other hand, living separately from Christ means stumbling in darkness and remaining ignorant of the glorious truths of God.

Living in darkness keeps us frustrated and chokes out the fullness of life which Christ desires for us. Darkness is death and pain. Jesus emphasized the horrific torment and frustration associated with darkness when He said in Matthew 8:12 that there will be "weeping and gnashing of teeth."

This frustration and torment is what a person experiences now in this life if they live independently of Christ, whether they are an unbeliever or an immature Christian. Paul told the Corinthians that they were still not mature enough to receive the meat of the Word. He referred to them as babies in Christ who can only have milk (1 Cor. 3:1-3).

Giving a steak dinner to a hungry infant will only frustrate him. Not only is he incapable of chewing the food, but he even lacks the coordination to cut the meat with a knife and fork. The child anguishes with hunger pains, but he can't be satisfied. Unless we mature as believers, we too will lead a frustrated existence. Refusing to grow spiritually will fence us off from every blessing now available to us. Also, rejecting the gospel and seeking other substitutes, will never satisfy the cravings which can only be met through Christ.

The Illumination of Christ

It is easy to be jealous over other people who seem to be triumphing in life. We see other marriages restored, friendships mended, financial troubles reversed. Instead of praising the Lord for their victories, we cry out to God, "Why can't this happen for me?"

Living on the outside of the abundant life is living in darkness and ignorance. It doesn't reflect lack of intelligence, but lack of illumination. The outpouring of Christ in our lives is available to everyone; it is a matter of revelation to remove the veil of cloudiness from our eyes. Jesus privately told His disciples in Luke 10:23, "Blessed are the eyes which see the things that ye see."

The illumination of Christ is brilliant. He can shine truth in every dark corner of our life, revealing His direction to us. We can think of it like a flashlight illuminating a dark country road. In an instant a traveler can see every pothole to step over as he moves in a direct route toward his destination.

The Bible is the written revelation of God, His Words transforming us and shedding light on our path. Also, worshiping with others who are walking in the light of His Word will bring even more understanding to us. The benefits of sharing with other committed Christians in a Bible-believing church should never be underestimated.

God will often place us in circumstances in which we are forced to see ourselves. During these times, we realize that we keep repeating the same mistakes or continue in the same pattern of thinking. We want to make better decisions and handle our problems more successfully, but we feel bound to our old ways.

Sometimes the Lord will place people across our path to challenge us or show us our area of darkness. It may be easy to discount their confrontation the first or even the second time, but it becomes harder to ignore the same comments from other people. Hearing about God's blessings is exhilarating, but hearing any kind of criticism is uncomfortable. Rather than forgetting about constructive comments, especially if confirmed by more than one person, it's better to consider that God might be shedding light on our life to transform us.

Through these experiences, God shows us that we need His light. In turn, we are driven to pore over His Word and allow it to shape our understanding of Him and the principles of His kingdom. Just like the morning sunlight forcing away the night, Jesus wants His revelation to dispel the darkness in our life.

Victory then comes to us. We are no longer slaves to our appetites and circumstances. Suddenly the scoreboard lights of our life are flashing triumph to the world. All this begins by choosing to receive what Christ has already provided.

Getting rid of spiritual ignorance is an ongoing process, and it isn't easy. On one occasion Leesa pointed out that two people said an action of mine had left a negative impression. I disagreed with their interpretation, but she explained that the two people didn't know each other and had come to the same conclusion. The fact was I resisted hearing the truth. I didn't want to hear about my faults, but my wife cared enough to tell me. I should have understood that God was using her to shed light on my path.

Spiritual Authority is Transferable

If we reject God's revelation in our lives, we will not grow and will pass on our immaturity to those we mentor. Whether we realize it or not, we either transfer darkness or light to others. This principle is plainly seen in a child who reflects his parent's ideas. Without even being conscious of this fact, he will even pick up their pattern of talking and facial expressions.

Whenever I see something in my children's lives I don't like, I can't blame my wife if she has been pointing out this same fault in me. We are always role models to others. We sometimes engage in wrong behavior, giving people the idea that what we are doing is an acceptable part of being a Christian. Instead of drawing others into the truths of God's kingdom, we transfer our ignorance without even knowing it.

God has created us to be a generational people, passing all that we are to our children and grandchildren, such as our language and our culture and our family history. The kingdom of heaven is no different. Our words and lives are constantly transferring the principles we live by.

The many Scriptures throughout the Old and New Testaments referring to Abraham, Isaac, and Jacob exhibit the principle of transferring spiritual authority. These three names representing three generations are presented collectively when mentioning God's covenant with the Jews. These men are also mentioned in Matthew 8:11, sitting down in the kingdom of heaven with many coming from the east and the west.

Transformation

God wants us to operate in a realm of faith which is far beyond how we have ever lived before.

When we are more concerned about serving others than we are concerned about ourselves, then we are living out God's love. Humility and selflessness transferred to others will transform lives. This kind of faith will raise us to a new level and will affect those around us. For example, have you ever extended kindness to someone who did not deserve it and watched how they were changed? Instead of arguing your point, you answered them gently and saw the truth of Proverbs 15:1 come to life: "A soft answer turneth away wrath."

Our problem is we won't allow God to change us. We are impatient and then attempt to create the transformation ourselves. We might try to increase our faith through works and legalism, or we might try to force spiritual growth upon others. An example of this would be someone trying to love and encourage their difficult spouse through their own feeble efforts, knowing this is how the Lord wants to turn him or her around. After a week or a month of no change, the person gives up and the relationship disintegrates.

The Israelites were too impatient in the desert to receive God's written Word. When Moses walked up Mount Sinai to meet with God, they decided they had waited long enough. They had Aaron create a golden calf to substitute for the living God (Exodus 32:1-4).

Having seen the Lord's power and provision did not produce true faith. They had seen God plague their enemy, part the Red Sea, and sustain them in the wilderness with manna and quail. They had tasted water which God had drawn from the desert rocks. They followed the glory of the Lord in the form of a cloud by day and light by night. Despite these experiences, their impatience impeded their partaking of the kingdom of heaven here on earth. They said no to His new template for living.

There is a time in our lives when God gives us a promise and we see it come to pass. Other times we hear the promise but we have to wait for its complete fruition. Maybe the Lord has impressed upon us that our finances are going to turn around, or our health is going to be restored, or a wayward son is going to return home. During these times we must place your confidence in the Lord and wait patiently upon Him.

Accept No Imitations

The Israelites thought they could bring about a new kingdom by turning to Aaron and doing things their own way, but this is impossible. There is a vast difference between what God brings and what we try to create ourselves. Any substitute we create can never replace what the Lord is able to give.

After Aaron had made the golden calf, the Israelites rose the next morning and presented offerings to their new god. Exodus 32:6 continues, saying they then "sat down to eat and to drink, and rose up to play." After creating a man-made answer for their spiritual needs, they celebrated, but their enthusiasm was misplaced. They were happy over a counterfeit.

We too can be deceived, rejoicing over an imitation. What God wants to give and what we are able to produce in ourselves is as far opposed as light is from dark.

Sometimes others see us heading in the wrong direction before we do. They warn us but we just don't want to hear it. Maybe they had grave reservations about our choice of a spouse.

All of their reasons were sensible, but we still felt they were wrong. Then after our painful marriage and divorce, we reflect back on those early days of courtship and remember what it was really like. All the conflicts which destroyed the marriage were present in the beginning when we dated.

Why didn't we see it? How were we deceived? Did we believe that God gave us a promise and this person had to be the fulfillment of that promise? We can avoid so much pain by relying upon God and not our feelings.

God wants to bring to pass for us what is already established in heaven. He wants to give us what is genuine and authentic. We cannot carry out God's plan using our old methods. If we try to achieve His work with our own efforts, we will be like the Israelites who corrupted themselves and skewed the plans of God.

Importance of Testimony

When God considered destroying the Israelites for their disobedience, Moses pleaded with Him to show mercy. He asked the Lord why He should harm His people, leaving way for the Egyptians to say He brought them out of Egypt just to kill them. In the end, Exodus 32:14 records, "The Lord repented of the evil which he thought to do unto his people."

This story in the Scriptures proves God's perspective on the importance of testimony and example to the unbelieving world. Ultimately, the Israelites were supposed to display the glory of God through their lives. If God destroyed them, the Egyptians would never hear about or know the fullness of God's provision for His people. They would only learn of the Lord's wrath and judgment. His goodness would be obscured, and His kingdom would not be transferred to the next generations.

Declaring God's Glory

We are to declare God's glory to the world and to transfer what God has done in our own lives to others, passing it from generation to generation. Following Jesus' pattern of discipleship, a spiritual father or mother would invest themselves into the lives of two or more people. As the younger believers mature, they too would disciple others. As more people come to Christ and transfer His authority to other believers, the kingdom of God multiplies.

The Lord wants His glory declared, recorded, and established in such fullness that the world will know He alone is the Lord of lords as expressed in Psalm 136:2-4. He who has overcome death and the world is in competition with no one.

The Scriptures clearly teach that Jesus has triumphed over all principalities and powers, and that He is now seated in heavenly places. So often we credit our struggles to the devil and his demons, when we are actually wrestling with our flesh. Some of what we call wickedness in high places is really just us. We simply get in the way of our own growth. Blaming the devil for our mistakes makes an excuse for our weakness and appeases our conscience as we continue in sin.

What a privilege it is to understand that God has His heart turned toward us, that His intentions for us are only good. How blessed it is that He chooses to establish His kingdom through us.

Discovering Your Weaknesses

We need a clearer understanding of God and who we are as His children. We should pray for the Lord to expose every corner of darkness in us and help us walk in His light. I'm not necessarily talking about sin. The darkness might be our old mind-sets which are inconsistent with who God wants us to be. These are also what the Scriptures mean as the old wineskins which cannot be filled with new wine.

We may not even be aware that we're walking in darkness. Although we're obedient to God, there is going to be some area of darkness that must be dispelled. All we have to do is ask the Lord to draw our attention to our areas of weakness. He may prick our conscience or direct our attention to a specific Scripture. Perhaps He will teach us through certain people and circumstances.

Once we are willing to recognize what needs to change, great things can happen. Divine transformation is possible. Ignorance can be replaced with the knowledge of the Lord. We can overcome enslaving habits and think through problems with the intuitiveness of God. The Lord can make us wise in all we say and do. When we go from darkness to light we become more than conquerors of ourselves and our circumstances.

The world can't help but take notice of this change because our life will resound with the declaration of God's glory. We will now be transferring light and not ignorance to this generation. People are hurting and waiting for us to bring them this kind of faith.

Do you realize that Jesus didn't need to be at the bedside of the centurion's servant in order to heal him? The centurion knew this. He said Jesus only had to speak the word and his servant would be healed. When Jesus heard this, He marveled at the man's faith, claiming He had not found such faith, even in Israel. Jesus' parting words were "Go thy way; and as thou hast believed, so be it done unto thee" (Matt. 8:13).

Our words can also go where our presence does not. We can transfer God's authority to others by explaining the power of Christ that is in them. Jesus says in John 14:12 that those who believe in Him will do even greater works.

We cannot afford to do as the Israelites did in the desert. We cannot settle for something we create. We must pursue what is true and genuine by waiting upon the Lord for His leading.

So, what's worse than waiting upon God? It's wishing that you had.

PART II

WHO AM I REALLY?

Discovering Don's Past

I couldn't put the Bible down after Don had showed me the Scriptures depicting Jesus. He had given me just enough of a taste that made me hungry for more. As I would read the passages more slowly, I began noticing what he meant. This mysterious man who seemed to have appeared from nowhere had given me a key to draw deeper truths out of the Bible. I had been reading and writing paraphrases but only gleaning general themes and story lines from the Scriptures. After only a few minutes with Don, I was discovering truths I could have never dreamed.

Don returned to my store the next day. From the window, I watched him pull up in a dilapidated red Buick.

"Good morning, Don," I said as he came inside.

"Hello, son." He smiled and sat in a chair near my counter. He was wearing the same soiled shirt and tattered trousers.

I couldn't help wondering if he knew how much he had stirred me with his teaching. I found myself asking him questions about Scriptures I had read but never understood. Over and over he showed me how the passages reflected Christ.

He laughed with delight over my enthusiasm. "It's just like the flaming sword, son, pointing the way to Jesus."

"How is it that nobody seems to see this?" I asked.

"They need to read it like they're doing it for the first time," he said. "You can't approach the Word of God bringing preconceived notions."

He said there were two kinds of people. One kind reads the Bible and it puts a burden on them. The other reads the Bible and they're released from their burden."

"Why the difference?" I asked.

"The one who is released by what he reads," he said, "sees the truth."

A couple of my friends came into the store. When they walked up to the counter I introduced Don.

They spoke to each other but I could tell Don was uncomfortable. I tried to draw him into our conversation, but he withdrew to another part of the store as if browsing for groceries. I didn't know if he felt like he was intruding into our conversation or maybe he was just ill at ease around people who dressed in business suits or who seemed somewhat affluent.

When my two friends left, Don came back to his chair and told me his story.

Fifty years earlier when he was in his twenties, he loved the church. He'd listen closely to every sermon and conversation that expounded upon Jesus. He wanted an intimate relationship with Christ and the abundant life the Lord talked about in the Scriptures.

During one church service Don couldn't stay in his seat any longer and went up to the altar. The pastor stepped from behind the pulpit and leaned toward him as the invitation hymn played. Don said that he wanted the fullness of Christ in his life. He wanted to receive the baptism of the Holy Spirit.

The pastor told him to confess his depravity and his filthiness. "Tell the Lord," he said, "how mean you are."

These words broke Don's spirit. He suddenly felt condemned and unworthy to receive anything good from the Lord.

Don never went up front to the altar again. The words of his pastor took root in his heart and their dark message seized his imagination. From then on he sat in the back of the church and left quickly at the end of every service. Whenever he now thought of the Lord he saw Him as the God of judgment whom he had to appease with good works.

Eventually, Don withdrew further from his church and began searching the Scriptures to discover the true person of Jesus.

A few years later Don married, but the relationship disintegrated. After he and his wife divorced he was completely devastated. He couldn't bear living apart from his wife and children. Around the same time, his diabetes worsened and he was forced to quit work. I could tell he still agonized over the loss of his wife.

Don cried as he told me this story. "After I lost everything," he said, "I ran to Jesus and made Him my companion."

Two boys came into the store about that time and began searching the shelf of candy.

Don pulled a stained handkerchief from his pocket, raised his glasses just enough to wipe his eyes and smiled at the children. "Sometimes it's hard to make a choice with all those flavors." He leaned down to where he was eye-to-eye with the boys and asked them what kind of day they were having.

I was struck at how much rapport he had with these kids. The boys told him about their ball game and their school and their dogs. They told him about their favorite teacher and what they dreamed of being when they got older. He laughed with them, hanging on their every word as if their stories were the best he'd ever heard.

I still didn't quite know what to think of Don, but I knew he had something that I wanted. He was helping me see the fullness of the Scriptures. He was showing me the true person of Christ, and this conflicted with most everything I had been taught.

I knew within two days after meeting him that I couldn't experience the abundant life Jesus promised by just hating who I was before I was saved. I had to understand who I was in the eyes of the Lord.

After the children left, I asked Don if he could come in regularly and show me more truths from the Scriptures.

"Sure, son," he said.

I gave him gas money, but he didn't want to take it.

"Please," I said. "It's important for me to see you every day."

"Beloved, now are we the sons of God, and it doth not yet appear what we shall be: but we know that, when he shall appear, we shall be like him; for we shall see him as he is."

1 John 3:2

Chapter Four

Understand You Are a Child in God's Family

Spiritual Families

God calls us his friends. How can we fathom the Creator of the universe desiring a relationship with you and me? However, this is exactly why he created us. He is drawing people through Christ to be part of His spiritual family. According to Ephesians 1:5, He adopts us as children because it is His pleasure to do so.

When we refer to each other as brothers and sisters in Christ, this is a true statement of our positions as believers with God being our heavenly Father. Thinking of ourselves as insignificant within the body of Christ is unbiblical. The Lord abounds in love, longing to bring all of us into His family and into fellowship with one another, each of us with an important part to play. We are the key to the development and expansion of the kingdom of God.

We must recognize that the growth of the church depends upon each of us maturing in our faith. Christ must be formed in every person. When we gather at church we are to consider it more than just a time to meet socially. We are coming together as a spiritual family for the encouragement of each other and for the increase of God's kingdom. The Lord cares about the ongoing transformation of believers. When Jesus talks about three servants receiving and investing their portion of talents in Matthew 25:19-29, He is teaching about different levels of spiritual growth.

As we mentor others, we become their spiritual father or mother as they become our spiritual sons and daughters. As the younger believers mature, they in turn become the spiritual parents to others. Before we can reach our full calling and experience God's complete empowerment, we have to understand this principle.

The Authentic Church

God can build His family through us if we will only live according to His truths. As the character of Christ shines in our lives, others will see the glory of this transformed life and want it for themselves. In this way, we should be advancing the kingdom of God with resounding victories in our circumstances and our relationships.

Not everyone will be healed and have every problem removed, but they will still be victorious. A believer can enjoy the settling peace of God through all of his trials and hardships, knowing the Lord has His hand on him. The unsaved people watching will see a difference in this kind of person, especially if he is surrounded and supported by Christian friends. The world should constantly see examples of God's love expressed in our lives during bad as well as good times. They should know that our relationship with Jesus gives us security.

There have been times when the church has offered a counterfeit. It may not have been planned this way, but the results are the same. When Christian worship services and meetings attract less people, we sometimes borrow from the world and incorporate sales techniques to draw a crowd. The powerful gospel of Christ becomes lost in a lot of fanfare and watered-down jargon. The sad part is that some people are attracted to this kind of packaging. However, this is a substitute for what is authentic and cannot succeed. The taste of this becomes bitter because it doesn't present a real Christ. When this format fails, churches can fall into the trap of thinking they just need a better program. They regroup, repackage the message, and start the failing process all over again.

Much of what we see today is the religious system that has been set up by man. The methods and rules which guide the conduct of churches may seem to contain the essence of Jesus, but they do not. Every church will have its own pattern of programs, but we must not think that this is necessarily reflecting Christ.

The true church is what God has been building since the resurrection of Jesus. It is not bound by the varying man-made systems and rules, for relationships are at the heart of it. True Christianity means having a vibrant relationship with our Holy Father and with each other. We are all to be committed to encouraging one another as we, according to Hebrews 12:1, "run with patience the race that is set before us."

Earning favor from each other by submitting to a man-made system cannot compare to what the Lord intends for His church. We must strive to understand the true Christ by meditating upon the Scriptures and listening to mature leaders. Otherwise, our understanding will never deepen beyond our preconceived notions or misinformation we've accepted in the past.

Not everyone has been nurtured in a loving home and can recognize healthy relationships, whether within families or within the church. Sometimes a person coming from a broken home will be attracted to a church promoting rules and rituals as the way to please God. They were raised in an environment where they had to earn their love and acceptance from their parents or siblings. When they find a church offering this same kind of dark philosophy, they think its right. People who are only familiar with criticism and abuse can make the mistake of attributing these traits to God.

The glorious truth is that Jesus completed everything for us at the cross. We don't have to beg God to love us. We don't have to fall into the anguishing habit of promising the Lord over and over that we'll do better to please Him. Instead, we understand what Jesus has done and who we are as His children. We simply raise our hands, open our mouths, and sing His praises.

I knew a businessman who was so cheap that he constantly made poor decisions. Instead of investing back into his business he would withhold the profit and miss a return for his money, much like the story of the man hiding his one talent. His employees who were never able to change him, jokingly said he was such a cheapskate that he would trip over a dime to pick up a nickel.

Sometimes we in the church are like this. We are looking for something in the distance, when what we need is right under our noses. We think we have to add to what Christ has already provided, when we haven't even yet experienced the fullness of life that Jesus has promised us.

The Danger

Jesus taught about the devil stealing the Word of God in His parable about sown seed falling by the wayside and on stony ground and among thorns. When the disciples questioned the meaning of His story, He asked how they can understand any of the parables if they don't understand this one (Mark 4:3-13).

What is so important about this particular parable? Why is its meaning paramount to their understanding of the kingdom of heaven?

In this story, Jesus exposes the dangers of the Word of God not taking root in our hearts. For example, someone newly saved might come to church and be moved by a sermon. They hear the Word of God and it touches their heart. They want to change their life and enjoy a more intimate relationship with the Lord. In this situation, the pastor successfully presented a message which encourages a young believer to see the need for a deeper commitment in their faith. The Word was sown like the seeds in the parable and received. Then come Monday, the worries of the young believer and his other pursuits take precedent over following Christ. Soon thereafter he is no longer seeking the Lord's direction because it just doesn't seem important.

Jesus' parable helps us understand the gravity of such a situation. It is a real spiritual battle where Satan steals the Word from us or the cares of this world choke it out of our lives.

We can receive God's message in a number of ways. The

seed of His Word can come to us through a conversation, a sermon, a hymn, or from reading the Bible and praying. Once we receive this revelation it changes our perspective. It might be a new understanding on how to treat our spouse or solve a particular problem or how to change the direction of our career.

The moment we receive God's Word, Satan will immediately try to steal it from us. On the other hand, some may hear the same message and not receive it, or even understand it.

On the very same day that the Lord told the parable of the sown seed, His disciples were shown the meaning of His teaching. That evening after taking a boat across the water, a great windstorm struck. While Jesus slept, the disciples panicked and cried out to Jesus, saying they were perishing. After Jesus rebuked the storm and it subsided, He asked them, "How is it that ye have no faith?" (Mark 4:35-40). The answer is they received His teachings, but allowed His Word to be stolen from their hearts. They became so swept up in their fear that they allowed the enemy to take away the very truths that could transform them.

This Parable Applied Today

How does this passage in Mark apply to us today? We too have a faithless and fearful generation. Like the disciples, we hear the truths of God, but we struggle to understand the mysteries of the kingdom. The problem is due to immaturity. We have suffered from a lack of nurturing because our spiritual fathers and mothers have failed their responsibility to mentor. Many families never attend church and hear the Word of God. Too many parents who do attend church never cultivate biblical truths at home. Prayer and meditation on Scripture are not an integral part of most Christians' lives.

As believers who are members in the family of God, we must reach out to each other. It's easy for the enemy to steal Sunday's biblical truth from a young Christian who finds himself alone on Monday. Churches receive calls frequently from believers who want a quick fix to straighten out their confused lives. Praying with them over the phone and encouraging them to come to the services is the first step. Ultimately, they need a mature Christian to take them under their wing and nurture them.

Can you imagine the result if thousands of people received the Word of God on Sundays and then were encouraged and prayed for throughout the week? Our spiritual fathers and mothers could teach the younger in Christ how to become grounded in the Scriptures. Surely this would defeat Satan's attempt to steal God's truths from His people.

The Challenge

When we do not allow the Word of God to change us, we are frustrated by our ignorance and lack of maturity. A lot of times this frustration leads people to abandon their church. When they see others as being victors in life while they are constantly struggling, they feel disconnected and too uncomfortable to stay.

Growing in our faith takes time. We can't allow ourselves to become discouraged. Paul explains the mystery of his victorious life in Galatians 2:20, saying, "I am crucified with Christ: nevertheless I live; yet not I, but Christ liveth in me." This means that when we get saved we receive the Spirit of God within us and so have

Christ inside of us. Jesus may not yet be fully formed due to our immaturity, but He is in us.

Luke 2:40 describes Jesus as a child maturing and growing stronger. Later in this same chapter it says, He "increased in wisdom and stature, and in favour with God and man" (Luke 2:52). When He was about thirty years old the Spirit of God descended upon Him at His baptism. If Jesus went through stages of development, we should also expect a similar pattern of growth.

Paul wrote to the Galatians about Christ forming in them as they mature. This same development must happen for every believer, with Jesus increasing in us and the person we are now decreasing. The wisdom we gain through God is something far different from our normal plotting and planning. It's not just a clever strategy of solving problems. Heavenly wisdom is breathed from the mouth of God.

We grow when we allow the seed of God's Word to take root in our hearts. As we meditate upon Scriptures and reflect upon what we've received in church, we can be transformed. Then as we encourage one another, our lives will bear fruit and increase the kingdom of heaven.

"The hand of the Lord was upon me . . ."

Ezekiel 37:1

Chapter Five

God Inspires
and Initiates

Waiting for Confirmation

Many of us want to change something in our lives. Maybe we need a new job. Maybe we need to turn around a family problem. Perhaps we need freedom from debt. As a believer we pray to God for an answer and our mind moves to many possibilities. Finally we feel God has revealed the correct direction, but we're not really certain. How do we know which course to take? How can we be sure we have the Lord's leading?

Most importantly, we must wait for confirmation from the Lord. If He is the One providing the answer, then He will confirm this to us.

There is nothing wrong with planning or assessing our options, but we must test the course of action against what the Bible says. For example, if we're praying that the Lord will send us a spouse, we must obviously find someone who is not married. Seeking a married person is not an option. The Bible, which is the revealed Will of God, commands that we honor the marriages of others. After praying and searching God's Word, then arriving at a decision, we should see if we then have peace over the matter. If we're still full of doubt and remain unsettled, we must wait.

Abraham's Promise

God promised Abraham a direct heir and descendants equal in number to the stars (Genesis 15:2-5). Abraham believed God but he didn't understand how it could happen since his wife, Sarah, was beyond child-bearing years. Instead of waiting upon the Lord's promise, Abraham tried to accomplish the results by having a child with Sarah's maidservant, Hagar. He did succeed in fathering a child but it brought much heartbreak (Genesis 16:1-16). He got ahead of God and suffered for it. Ultimately God did fulfill His promise and gave Abraham and Sarah a son named Isaac (Genesis 21:1-3). However, Abraham could never change the fact that he had another son, Ishmael, through his wife's handmaiden and would always have to deal with this choice.

Not waiting upon the Lord for direction will cause problems. Sometimes our impatient acts in the flesh seem necessary to bring in God's promises, but they always fail. Abraham's efforts did produce a child, but it wasn't the heir God had promised. There is no way we can match what blessings God has in store for us.

As we search for solutions to our problems, we must know that God will give direction through His Spirit. We must be convinced that our Lord who inspires and makes promises is the same One who provides. Sarah's advanced age with all of its limitations could not impede the promise of God. We need to discern the difference between God saying, "Now" and God saying,

"Wait". Understanding this will change our lives. Otherwise, we will create messes for ourselves over and over again.

The fact that Jesus grew in wisdom supports the idea that our Lord was teachable. As Christ develops within us, we too should display a teachable spirit. The day that we think we cannot learn anymore is the day we stop growing.

Being overly critical of others can prevent the Lord from speaking to us, whether through a sermon or a conversation. The Lord may also bring an answer to us through a person talking about something completely unrelated to our problem. I don't know of any person who has asked the Lord for guidance and heard Him bellow the answer through the heavens. Instead, most people get answers in ways that may be quite ordinary but which are spoken from God nonetheless.

Proverbs 15:31 emphasizes the importance of listening, saying, "The ear that heareth the reproof of life abideth among the wise." A person who doesn't listen and who is more concerned about sharing their own testimony, will often miss what God may be trying to tell them through someone else. We all have done this, hoping for someone to hurry through their story so that we can share ours.

One evening only an hour before having to leave for a speaking engagement, I received a call from a man wanting to discuss his problems he was having with his church. At first, I didn't mind this interruption because I felt more than prepared for my message. But then the conversation labored on. After fifteen minutes I felt completely drained and I tried to politely end the conversation. Suddenly I recognized the Lord was showing me through this man's words what was supposed to be at the heart of my sermon. Through what would be considered commonplace, God had orchestrated this interruption for my good and for the benefit of those who would be hearing my message. I learned a good lesson on expecting God to speak through the ordinary.

Christ Formed In Us

We all need to be open to the Lord as He molds and shapes us, cultivating a heart to hear God's soft voice. When the Lord sends someone across our path, we should be vigilant to see if they have a nugget of truth to share. If we're exposed to someone's ungodly behavior, we need to ask ourselves if the Lord is providing us with a mirror of sorts to view our own life. This kind of reflection can be both sobering and life-changing.

If we want to enter into the blessings of God and understand the mysteries of His kingdom, we must allow Christ to be formed in us. Through this we can gain a vision of what the future holds and a glimpse of what it can be through the empowerment of the Holy Spirit. God can reveal to us our direction and our gifts. We may not yet be walking in the fullness of this vision, but we will begin to see it.

When God begins to show us our true spiritual identity, it is exciting because He is preparing us for a new direction. Sometimes we encounter a person who is frustrated by such an experience. Rather than being excited about where God will take them, they are upset at not yet being there. They need to be encouraged, knowing God will continue leading them if they only continue moving toward their destination.

God will bring us through life's events and make us better than we were. He doesn't abandon us to sickness or a divorce or to the sadness of losing a loved one. Instead, He walks us through it all, never forsaking us. And, if we allow Him, He will help us grow and mature in Christ through our suffering.

Have you ever found yourself in a situation or problem that you didn't cause, completely dumfounded to how it happened? This can be painful because we tend to torment ourselves, wondering how we could have done things differently. We do create our own problems with bad decisions, but sometimes trouble comes our way through no fault of our own. Especially during these times we have to learn that suffering develops the character of Christ in us.

Understanding Suffering

Not only does our pain cause us to lean on the Lord and grow in Him, but it also equips us to help others. No one is exempt from the challenges of life, for the Bible tells us that the rain falls on the just and the unjust. Some of the greatest saints of God have suffered terrible atrocities. Frankly, suffering is inescapable. As we mature we will increase in our capacity to help others through such times, to guide them through the dark hour that is theirs for a season. We won't ever become an effective father or a mother in the Lord until we understand how suffering deepens our empathy for people so that we can minister to them.

As a pastor, I have seen too many times immature Christians trying to help others understand their problems. Often they lead people in a wrong direction. Having a limited understanding of God's Word, they draw ridiculous conclusions about God withholding His love or sending the problem. Their attempts to encourage individuals are fruitless because their comments are not in keeping with God's Word. They commiserate without bringing enlightenment. Instead of this becoming a time of growth for the one in need, their suffering is intensified because they cannot discover the loving presence of God.

When we begin to understand that Christ forms in us through suffering, we have peace. We have God's perspective on our situation and can see what He can accomplish. Instead of doing everything we can to avoid the suffering, we choose to embrace it. Since we cannot change our circumstances, we try to understand what the Lord wants us to learn.

With this new perspective, God begins to change our character. In time we resolve to shed every hindrance which blocks our relationship with God. We want to change. When we recognize areas which we're incapable of changing, we then lean more into Him for help. This can be the biggest blessing arising out of our personal struggles because we realize that only God can win our battles. When we abandon our self-righteous attitude and trade our meager efforts in for the mighty works of our God, our situations are more than improved. Most importantly, we become transformed. Suffering is like working out at the gym, building muscle and strength and developing endurance.

Effective Kingdom Builders

1 Corinthians 11:28 exhorts each person to examine themselves. This means taking a personal inventory of our character under the microscope of God's Word. Looking honestly

at ourselves helps us recognize which traits and habits we need to keep and which we must toss out.

As well as examining ourselves, it is also prudent to listen to the assessment of others whom we trust. Usually, a compassionate mentor can see more in our life than we can.

I know from experience that most of the time I never see the fullness of my circumstances or mistakes even when I'm completely impacted by them. After struggling and complaining, it still takes someone close to me finally bringing insight into my problem. It is then that I see my situation through their eyes and understand the truth. This kind of revelation can help a person break a pattern of living which has been producing anguish for a lifetime.

It is true that we *live* life forward but *learn* life backward. When we review a situation in the past, we can see it more clearly than when we're in the middle of it.

Effective kingdom builders know the importance of having a group of believers to whom they are accountable. Whether a Sunday School class or a Bible cell group, people with a heart for Christ can lift us spiritually. They can help us recognize when we are walking in the flesh or warn us when we get out of line. They rally around us during troubling times and help us navigate through life's murky waters. Also, these brothers and sisters in Christ become accountable to us.

The Body of Christ is commanded to act in this way, not to heap guilt on each other, but to encourage one another. Together, we also celebrate times of growth and increase in wisdom. True followers of Jesus are thrilled over the victories of other believers.

They want the kingdom of God expanded in the lives of their spiritual brothers and sisters.

Conversely, having no Christian support group can only make us feel isolated and helpless. The result will be a skewed perspective on God's answers, most likely leading to frustration and blaming others for our problems.

We all must surround ourselves with people who love the Lord. We must cultivate Christian relationships daily, not solely for our needs but also to help others.

Victorious Life

When we are inspired on Sunday by a message or song or testimony, then we must walk in it on Monday. The real victory is not simply God giving us His Word because He is always doing this through personal revelation and through the Bible. The real victory comes from us living out His truths. When the problems attack the peace of God we received on Sunday, we know how to respond.

It is never easy facing a difficulty. Whether it is sickness or family trouble or financial loss, sometimes we feel like we've been knocked down, left on the ground with the breath knocked out of us. In this state it's hard figuring out a solution or understanding how the circumstances are going to benefit us in the long run. We may feel we've done everything we know to do and everything is still caving in around us. We want to be strong in the Lord, but we are so weak. During these times we can only cry out for God to do something.

If we really want to see the manifestation of the sons of God and see the Lord's anointing released in the lives of people, we must challenge our minds with the truth of the Scriptures. Too often we come to church to hear sermons which affirm us and make us feel good. We may be uncomfortable hearing messages which spiritually stretch us, but they will benefit our lives. When we are confronted with our sinful motivations and wrong behavior, we have the opportunity to change before we slip further down into trouble and pain.

James 1:2-4 clearly expresses the positive impact of understanding our troubles, saying, "My brethren, count it all joy when ye fall into divers temptations, knowing this, that the trying of your faith worketh patience, but let patience have her perfect work, that ye may be perfect and entire, wanting nothing."

Instead of feeling broken when we wrestle with temptation, we are to be joyful. Instead of being anxious, we are to be calm because something good will come out of the circumstances. We are to allow patience, a fruit of the Spirit of God, to complete its work in us. When we know this truth as James says, we will feel peace through every trial, knowing it will change us for the better.

Few people will shout out "Hallelujah!" when hearing a message about enduring suffering. Nevertheless, we mature through trials and struggles. This is how we are challenged to draw upon the strength of the Lord. We forget ourselves and seek God and His answers through His Word.

Being Challenged

When the hearts and minds of a congregation are influenced by God's Word, they will have a new spirit and worship will take on new meaning. This change will extend to their homes and workplaces, spilling over into their families and neighborhoods. The manifestation of Christ in their lives will be apparent everywhere.

In time, we will see the expansion of God's kingdom has never been limited to a building or a Sunday. The Lord will show Himself wherever we go. The ones who recognize and understand these mysteries will be those who persevere in the kingdom.

Are we going to be a group of people who see and hear, but never understand? Or, are we going to believe and be ushered into a deeper relationship with our King?

Jesus showed us through His example that we must preach to the poor and the downtrodden. He came to draw in the people who are broken. He came to free the captive, heal the sick, and restore sight to the blind. His message was never accepted by the "religious" who felt they had all the answers.

With Christ formed in us, we are equipped to help the hurting. There are many in need in whom we must deposit the Word of God and whom we must help guard against the Enemy. We know Satan wants to steal every truth from them before it takes root in their heart. We must always be ready to serve others in this capacity as Jesus did.

We all have met people who want nothing to do with the gospel. They openly reject anything shared about Christ. We must never quit praying for them, but we cannot spend all our time trying to convince those who forever resist the truth. Most certainly we must seek out the poor in spirit who know they need a Savior. When we find those hungry for the gospel, we cannot resort to advancing the kingdom of God by our own efforts. Instead, we must proceed in the power of God, going in His direction and accomplishing His plans. Whenever we try to coerce and cajole people into faith we will only fail and wear ourselves out. Instead, we need to live out the gospel message before people and love them.

Someone once said it correctly: people don't care how much you know but rather how much you care.

PART III

WHAT DO I CHOOSE?

WATCHING DON CHANGE

Leesa was convinced Don was a blessing sent to me for a definite purpose. She pointed out the fact that he had come into my life just one month after the civil suit was brought against me. I agreed.

When I told my Bible study group about Don, I could tell some were a little skeptical. The more I explained about his appearance and his understanding of the Scriptures, the more farfetched my tale seemed.

I drove home that night with Leesa, realizing that I couldn't really blame anyone who was suspicious of my story. When I was away from the store and thinking about this stranger who had suddenly come into my life, even I could hardly believe it.

The next morning I left an hour early for work and tried to locate Don's house. I had never requested a specific address that first day, so I thought I would drive up and down the particular route he had mentioned on his credit application and search for his red Buick.

I drove slowly but never found his car.

The road narrowed and led deeper into a hollow of shanties and yards littered with debris. Eventually the surface of the country lane got worse with potholes and collapsed shoulders around the curves. Still not finding his car, I decided to end my search and go to work.

When Don came into the store that day I asked him where he lived. "I was out on your road but never saw your Buick."

His countenance dropped. I could see he was embarrassed.

"I'll tell you, son," he said. "It may not be the kind of place you'd expect."

He hesitated like he didn't really want to explain, and I didn't know what to say.

"It's just a small shack without any water or electric," he said. "Somebody's just letting me live there."

I knew then I should never ask him about it again.

One evening just before closing, an elderly woman from the nearby high-rise called in for a small delivery of groceries. I was always happy to provide this service after work but this particular evening I had a commitment shortly after work and couldn't spare much time. As Don helped me box up the items I told him how I was really rushed.

"I'll deliver the groceries," he said.

"You don't mind?"

"Not at all, son," he said. "I'd be glad to."

I thanked him as he left with the order.

The next day Don told me how he had struck up a conversation with the woman in the high-rise and her neighbor. "Lovely people up there," he said. "I really enjoyed taking her the groceries."

From then on Don became my delivery person. I paid him and gave him extra gas money. I didn't ask him to clean up or change his appearance. I just let him deliver as he was with no apologies. When orders came he boxed them up and left in his old red Buick. I always knew when he was returning because of the familiar rattle of his engine.

In between deliveries he and I seemed to talk about everything. He was able to expound in depth on any book in the Bible. I began writing down questions for when I'd see him the next morning or when he returned from dropping off orders.

Don loved people. He talked of this often. He had a gentle spirit and customers, especially the elderly and the young, were drawn to him. After watching him kneel down to look eye-to-eye at the two boys buying candy that second day, I noticed that he did this with every child. He delighted in their enthusiasm and wanted to hear their stories. He laughed heartily with the old and the young, and he cried over their hardships.

He talked often with me about the importance of family.

"Treasure your wife and children," he'd tell me. "Be willing to lay your life down for them. When your babies look to you to hold them, then hold them."

Over the next few months Don made friends with the residents in the high-rise where he delivered groceries. He began driving them to doctor's appointments or picking up their medication.

One morning Don came to work with his hair cut and his beard shaved. He had on the same old shirt and tattered pants, but they had been washed. I was careful not to say too much to him about the change. We just continued enjoying each other's company, and he continued delivering groceries.

A few days later he came to work wearing a new red button-down plaid shirt and pair of jeans. He told me he was now leading Bible studies with his friends at the high-rise.

Don's shyness around some of the more affluent customers slowly dissipated. He seemed more confident around them, talking with them freely as he did with the children and the elderly.

Everybody loved him. Customers began bringing him gifts, whether a shirt or a pair of shoes, but never out of pity. No one was giving with the purpose of providing for a poor person. Instead, they just wanted to express how much they valued him.

Then one day Don told me he was changing residences. "I'm moving into the high-rise," he said.

"When I was a child, I spake as a child,
I understood as a child, I thought as a child:
but when I became a man, I put away childish things."
1 Corinthians 13:11

Chapter Six

GROWING UP AND MATURING IS A PERSONAL CHOICE

Increasing in Wisdom

Once upon a time we all were children with limited understanding, relying upon others for our safety and sustenance. We acted and talked like a child and had limited influence. Such is characteristic of this time of life, but it is only for a season until we grow and mature into adults. At some time we are expected to take our place in the world as citizens, spouses, and diligent workers in chosen careers.

Jesus also came into this world as a child, gradually maturing into adulthood. The few verses about Jesus' youth refer to His growth and development of certain traits. He wasn't simply born as an adult. At different times in this life he was an infant, an adolescent, a teenager, and a young adult.

Our spiritual life is similar. We come to God with limited understanding, eventually increasing in wisdom and influencing others. Our goal should be to grow in Christ so that we may influence others for the Lord's kingdom.

Becoming Mature Kingdom Builders

Did you know that it is God's will for us to mature and become all He wants us to be? The first step is committing our life to Christ and knowing we have been adopted into the family of God. Then we must actively follow the Lord's direction. Growing in the Lord is a personal choice, and we must deeply desire to grow in wisdom and understanding.

Every detail of our background, where we were born and who we had as parents, didn't come about by chance. God uses it all to shape us. He molds us with every experience, even the bad ones. For example, God can build strength in someone coming out of a broken home. Maybe a child of divorced parents will become a peacemaker for others in conflict. Maybe a woman who has suffered from an abusive husband will teach other girls what qualities to seek in a mate. Wisdom gained in the fire of a bad experience can better our lives and equip us to help others.

Jesus also had parents and a background. As he grew from an infant He had the experience of being part of a family and living in a community as we do. Jesus knows all about temptation and the daily struggles because he lived on earth just as we do. The difference was He had no sin.

After the Spirit of God descended upon Him like a dove and God proclaimed Him as His Son in whom He was well pleased, Jesus began His ministry (Matt. 3:16-17, 4:17). Everything that happened up to this point prepared Him. Jesus' purpose was confirmed by the Father and so He went forth with the work of the kingdom.

Jesus didn't waste time debating theology with religious people. Instead, He displayed His relationship with God as He reached out to the poor and broken-hearted. He knew why He had come to earth and never wavered from His mission.

God will also send us to reach those who are poor in spirit, those who know they need Jesus. At the same time, Satan will attempt to impede our ministry by sending others who don't want to hear the gospel. These people will want to debate everything we say. Rather than argue, it is better to continue to pray for them and turn our attention to the ones ready to hear the Word. Fruitless debate won't succeed in drawing scoffers into the kingdom. It will only distract us from our purpose by wasting our time and draining us emotionally.

The Character of Christ

As we grow in wisdom and maturity in Christ, a number of things can distract us from our calling. Sometimes the details of day-to-day life get in the way or challenges arise or a crisis suddenly breaks out.

To avoid getting sidetracked, we must develop a sensitivity to the Spirit's leading and understand our role in the kingdom of God. Once we take our eyes off the Lord, our thoughts and direction are thrown off balance. We may even become distracted by activities that are related to church but do not cultivate our relationship with God. Family and church and all the basic responsibilities of life deserve our attention, but none of it can replace communing with Christ.

We often hear in the media about the importance of equality, fairness, and justice. These qualities spring forth from the heart of God. As the character of Christ is formed in us we will display these virtues in our lives. When this happens, political correctness will fall in the face of what is true. What is right will be declared as right, and what is wrong will be declared as wrong. As this happens, God's perspective will be displayed across the earth by His people. It will be as stated in Amos 5:24, saying: "Let judgment run down as waters, and righteousness as a mighty stream."

God gives us His word, whether a blessing or a promise, and then provides some form of illustration to clarify our understanding. Just as He exhibited the parable of sown seed to his frantic disciples when he calmed the storm, the Lord will show us something. It might be a sermon or something we read, but we will receive confirmation. God's goal is to implant His truth into our heart. Our head and heart must be in agreement. When this occurs, that promise or that blessing becomes a part of us. Jesus was showing the disciples that when our head and our heart agree, we are then operating in faith, not fear.

Releasing Dominion to Others

Learning to live by faith is important. Once we learn to do this we can then release it into the lives of other people. We can only give to others what we already have. Nobody is interested in listening to someone about living by faith if they don't walk it out themselves. People going through a difficult time need someone who can stand with them and help them. When we operate in faith we do not strive because we are relying upon the Lord.

I'm one of those people who likes to initiate. I am assertive. If I get my hands and eyes on something, I'll pursue it. You may be the same way. I'm talking about spiritual pursuits, not material gain. For example, when God places someone's spiritual growth on my heart, I want to see the fulfillment happen now. I want to see that person come into the prosperity of the kingdom this very day. Impatience makes me want everything to happen rapidly. I have learned that when I try forcing results out of God, I'm not trusting Him to do the best. Like a child with limited understanding, I am making demands of Him.

Lucifer the Thief

Lucifer began as a son of God and then became the Lord's enemy. Now he wants to steal from man all that God has given. We read in the Old Testament how he destroyed Job's wealth, children, and health (Job 1:12-21, 2:6-7). The devil knew he could hurt God by deceiving Adam, and this has been his ongoing strategy. After the fall in the Garden of Eden, Adam not only suffered separation from the Lord, but God's work was thwarted. This catastrophe came after God had commanded Adam in Genesis 1:28 to "Be fruitful, and multiply, and replenish the earth." Now Adam was separated from his loving Father and feeling like an orphan.

Jesus came to remove our position of alienation. We are not to feel as orphans but know through Christ we are the sons and daughters of God. An orphan mind-set is the antithesis of God's true view of us. We are to walk in full confidence because we know the Lord's intentions toward us are always good.

The Prodigal Son

The story of the prodigal son in chapter 15 of Luke illustrates our position in the kingdom of God. In this passage, the son knew of his inheritance and felt he had the right to it. Rather than waiting to receive what was rightfully his, he demanded that his father give it to him immediately.

We sometimes approach God in this same way. We may actually know the Lord is going to bring something to us, maybe a particular job or ministry, but we are too impatient to wait. We foolishly feel we know more than God. We aren't happy with His time frame and want to bring about our blessings faster.

After the prodigal son took his inheritance, he left his home and squandered his money foolishly. When a famine depleted the land, poverty and hunger forced the son to find work tending pigs. Covered in mud and slop, he resorted to eating the husks that he fed the animals. Finally, the pain of his circumstances sobered him to the realization that he was much better off living in his father's home. He declared to himself, "How many hired servants of my father's have bread enough and to spare, and I perish with hunger!" He then decided to go to his father and tell him he has sinned and wants to return home. He planned to beg his way back by becoming a servant because he no longer felt worthy to remain a son.

We too sometimes take on this mind-set of an orphan. We may attend every church service, pray daily, and even witness for the Lord, but all under a dark cloud of feeling alienated from God. We live out our lives with the spirit of an orphan and so never produce the fruit that the Lord intends.

The glorious part of the prodigal parable is the father's reaction to the return of his son. When he saw his boy from a distance he was overwhelmed with love, raced to him, and kissed him. His son could never finish his rehearsed speech about becoming a servant because his father rejoiced, declaring, "My son was dead, and is alive again; he was lost, and is found." The father demanded that the servants bring the best clothes and choicest calf to celebrate. This excitement was not over the return of an orphan or even a backslidden son. The exuberance of the father was over his son who was dead and now alive.

When we carry the spirit of an orphan we are living in the death of our trespasses and sins without even realizing it. This doesn't mean we're spiritually damned. It simply means we're not walking in the victory that God has given us. The prodigal son was lost, and then found. What did he find? He discovered his right standing with His father. If we want to grow in Christ we will need to understand our position as a child of our heavenly Father.

When the older brother in the parable came from the field and heard the music and dancing, a servant explained to him about the celebration and he burned with jealousy. He confronted his father about the lavish treatment of his brother. He said he was always the faithful son while his young brother lived recklessly. He complained further, saying his father never blessed him with such a celebration.

An orphan spirit produces jealousy over another's blessing. The elder son's comments to his father are similar to someone touting that they deserve more than someone else because of their many years of serving God. They may feel owed because they were the founding fathers of a church. They might argue, "You don't understand. I never missed a Monday night prayer meeting and was the dependable one. When everybody else turned their back on the pastor, I stood with him."

Comparing ourselves to another when we feel slighted is not productive. The elder brother compared himself to his brother to show how he was cheated. This very practice reveals the orphan spirit. We need to see ourselves as the son or daughter of the Most High God and our jealousy will dissipate.

When the father addressed his eldest boy in the parable, he confirmed his position as well by calling him "son." He went on to say "thou art ever with me, and all that I have is thine."

Can you imagine always being with our Father wherever we go? This is what this parable is telling us. Even through our mistakes and troubles, God is always with us. His love never changes. Everything in the heavenly places is ours. The father in the story doesn't tell his son, "Some of what I have is yours." He tells him he has it all.

The Giver of Good Things

Matthew 7:11 expands upon God's desire to bless us, saying, "If ye then, being evil, know how to give good gifts unto your children, how much more shall your Father which is in heaven give good things to them that ask him?"

Maybe, even as you read this, you are seeking escape from a problem or situation. It's not wrong examining different options to alleviate trouble as you pray over the matter. However, in the midst of our struggles we must understand that every trial and tribulation has the potential to form Christ in us. If we walk in faith through the matter it can take us from manifesting the spirit of an orphan to manifesting the spirit of a son. Those around us will notice that we have peace instead of despair, that we have victory instead of defeat.

Our natural inclination is to feel like an orphan because of Adam's fall. His disobedience separated him from God and gave us an orphan mind-set by default. This broken sense of self came with the original sin and was passed down to us.

God, however, has a remedy. Adam left us separated from God, but Jesus came to restore us. Christ made the way for us to unite with our Father, and so we no longer have to feel alienated from God. His work on the cross made it possible to banish our alienation and to become the children of God.

The Cross

There are lessons we can learn at the cross. The first is that Jesus submitted completely to His Father's will. Can you imagine that Christ came to earth with the end purpose of suffering and dying? He knew this was our only answer for spiritual restoration and He willingly submitted to the horrors of this death. Sometimes we are faced with experiences that can transform us only if we submit to the process.

It isn't easy walking in a place where there is pain. Even Jesus acknowledged this when he questioned the disciples in Mark 10:38, asking, "Can ye drink of the cup that I drink of, and be baptized with the baptism that I am baptized with?" He knew at this time the humiliation and death that He was soon to face.

We all want to enjoy the benefits of obeying God, but we don't want to endure the trials required to receive His glory. When we walk by faith we are trusting Him to guide us through these hardships and to bring us into His purpose.

Not For Sale

In the book of Acts, Philip preached to the people of Samaria, performing miracles of healings and casting out demons. In this same place a sorcerer named Simon who had been bewitching people for years heard Philip and became a believer. After he was baptized he followed Philip and was amazed at his performance of signs and miracles. Later when Simon saw people receiving the Holy Spirit through the apostle's laying on of hands, he offered money to buy this power for himself. Ultimately Peter rebuked him for not having the right perspective, thinking that a gift of God can be purchased.

An interesting aspect of this story is the fact that Simon never offered to buy from Philip the power to perform miracles and signs. Instead, he was more interested in the power he witnessed through Peter and John. Why didn't he prefer the ability to heal diseases and to cast out unclean spirits? Apparently he saw more value in receiving the Holy Spirit than in performing any miracle. His perspective about buying this power was skewed, but he did recognize the greatness of transforming people and equipping them to expand the kingdom of heaven on earth.

We can bring about the transfer of the kingdom of God from one person to another. Have you ever wondered why Jesus healed people and sometimes told them not to tell anyone? However, He never discouraged people from preaching His gospel. The fact that the Lord encouraged some to conceal their personal healing shows the kingdom of God is not confined to these manifestations. While signs and miracles are wonderful, our primary concern must be for the growth of the kingdom within us and outside of us.

We can't be obsessed with seeking miracles and ignoring the character of Christ and the building of His kingdom. Jesus knew there were many coming only for healings and not for receiving Him.

Jesus brought the glory of His kingdom to us through His suffering and His selflessness. Only through His death and resurrection could we be restored. The fact that suffering brings life can be seen in the apostles who were victorious through persecution and martyrdom. Each could have deserted Christ like Judas Iscariot, but they chose to follow the Lord. Others saw the authenticity of their commitment which never wavered in the face of death.

We sometimes find ourselves in debilitating circumstances from which we are trying to escape. We pray and feel assured that God's answer is for us to move on. After doing everything we know to do, it seems we hit road block after road block. For example, we might be stuck in a job and every opportunity to change is squelched. The Enemy will convince us that we aren't right with God or He never spoke to us about seeking new employment. He will spin any kind of lie to make us feel isolated and alienated from our heavenly Father.

Instead of making a demand of God, we need to nail our circumstance to the cross of Christ and ask God to teach us. When

Jesus died on the cross the paradox was then, and is now, that death brought life. Maturing in God is not always easy or pleasant. Once we understand that God has our best interests at heart, we can rest in Him and walk by faith rather than by sight. We know then in the very core of our being that we are His children. We can transfer the kingdom to others and know that even through adversity God will triumph.

*"Make no friendship with an angry man;
and with a furious man thou shalt not go."*

Proverbs 22:24

Chapter Seven

SELECT FRIENDS WISELY

A True Friend

There is no substitute for a true friend. According to Proverbs 18:24, "A man that hath friends must show himself friendly: and there is a friend that sticketh closer than a brother." When the Scriptures talk about a friend the word means someone who will stand with you through trouble. This kind of person will wait up late with you in a hospital or share their home during your financial crisis or look after your children when you're sick.

A true friend brings light into a dark situation, but a false friend brings hardship. We must carefully select those with whom we keep company. The values of people, good or bad, influence our lives. Someone full of Christ will bring us closer to Him. On the other hand, a self-centered person will dispel immaturity and darkness.

We tend to surround ourselves with people who tell us exactly what we want to hear. We'd rather be around those who agree with us, telling us we're always right. This kind of relationship is stagnating because it never encourages growth. The truth of the matter is our choice of friends is a deliberate action, often reflecting how we wish to be.

Conversely, we can surround ourselves with those who are spiritually mature. Rather than just telling us what we want to hear, a Christian mentor will tell us what we need to hear. With their guidance we can gain insight on our struggles and how we should walk in the light of God. This healthy relationship will challenge us to become better and will lead to us bearing fruit.

When we are feeling down or find ourselves in a difficult place, we need encouragement and prayer. During these times we need someone who will tell us what the Bible teaches. Without this proper direction we can fall prey to Satan's lie that we're unloved and unworthy of God's blessings.

The Lord is Always With Us

When one of my daughters was four years old she had to have surgery. She remained calm until it came time for her to be moved to the operating room. When she realized the moment had come, she panicked with tears welling up in her eyes. Leesa and I had planned all along to stay with her until she was under anesthesia so she wouldn't feel alone. When the doctors and several nurses arrived, we were told we couldn't go into the operating room. I explained to them that I had promised my daughter that I'd stay with her, but they politely explained it was against the hospital's policy.

My daughter only knew she was surrounded by strangers in a foreign place and was being wheeled away from her parents. Leesa and I stood helpless, holding hands and praying, while our daughter looked back with tears streaming down her cheeks.

My daughter may have felt abandoned, but she wasn't. My wife and I were only a room away, just counting the minutes when we could see her. This experience was painful for our daughter but it was for her good. Without this particular surgery she would be facing problems twenty years later. In time, of course, the anguish was over and years later she appreciated the importance of this care.

As Christians we often respond to difficult situations like this. When we don't see God working through our circumstances we quickly conclude that He has abandoned us. We might be crying out to God because of a struggling marriage or financial problems, wondering when His help will come. We might be battling problems that we've created, beating ourselves against the current, trying to change everything when we can't. Then we finally just want to escape from our problems. We only want to run and hide.

The truth is that the Lord is always with us. He sees where we are, knowing every problem we're facing. He will not forsake us because of who He is and what we mean to Him.

While I watched the medical staff roll my daughter away for the operation, the Lord impressed upon me the thought that He wants the best for His children. Like my daughter's limited understanding about her surgery, we may not know that trials will help us, but they do. Trouble transforms us to become better. If we endure and do not abort this process, we will grow and change.

Purpose of Ministry

We must surround ourselves with mature believers who

understand the purpose of trials. Someone who is not grounded in God's Word will only encourage escape from our situation, whether from a unhappy marriage or a broken friendship. They will not see the importance of persevering or understand the glory of restoration. However, people seeking the direction of God will support us during struggles and be better at understanding the benefit of enduring. Spiritual parents can help sharpen our vision of right choices.

As we mature, our authority over circumstances will increase. We don't have to be subject to the problems which trouble others. As we are transformed into the person God intends for us to be, we expand our dominion over unrighteous appetites and entangling habits. Even our ability to think is enhanced because we are taking on the mind of God. This level of maturity equips us to help others endure their challenges.

Hiding past sins and struggles from the church will not encourage other believers. Sometimes we want to forget from where we came. After we're saved, we don't want others thinking of us as the drug addict or thief or gossip we once were. Concealing our past and pretending it never happened won't help those around us who are presently struggling with the same problems.

There are people in our midst who are too embarrassed to ask for our help. If they know about our victories, they will know they too can find victory. They will know that we understand their problems intricately because we have suffered in the same way. Unless we are willing to open our hearts to each other, the church will only be a façade of righteous people who don't need each other.

Simply put, unless we give our testimony how will anyone

know what God did for us? How will people know what God can do for them?

Someone struggling with alcohol or drugs needs to hear our story about God replacing our aching addiction with His refreshing Spirit. Those enslaved to years of welfare need to hear how the Lord guided our steps and increased our prosperity. Parents depressed over wayward children need to know how God intervened in drawing our children back into His favor.

The purpose of the ministry is for all of us to share our lives and to encourage each other to partake of the kingdom of heaven. Instead, most congregations expect the pastor to minister to all the hurting people. How can we expect to operate as the Body of Christ with this traditional pattern?

God's plan is for everyone to minister to each other by openly sharing their lives. Young believers may resist growth. Instead they may only desire confirmation that they are good enough. If we expose them to the glorious benefits of committing their lives to Christ, they will draw nearer. If we stop short of this, we abort what God wants to do in their lives as well as ours.

Needing Each Other

We believers need to be closely involved with each other so that we may learn and grow. Church should be the place where we are taught and fed the truths of God. Paul tells the Christians in the book of Hebrews that they need to be taught again when they actually should have matured into teachers. They still need the milk of the Word when they should be ready for the meat. He explains in Hebrews 5:13-14 that "every one that useth milk is unskilful in the word of righteousness: for he is a babe. But strong meat belongeth to them that are of full age, even those who by reason of use have their senses exercised to discern both good and evil."

There are some sitting in church who feel the sermons are for everybody else. They may complain that they didn't gain anything from the teaching or maybe couldn't even understand it. The sermons they admit to understanding might prompt them to wish others got it. "I wish so-and-so were in church to hear this," they might say. "I'm getting a copy of this tape and leaving it in their car."

Are these comments familiar? This kind of attitude blinds us to truth and results in us missing the very message meant for us. Truths from the Lord are meant to guide us during particular times. His Words are to help during specific seasons.

Only a comparison with food (milk and meat) can capture the importance of God's teaching. Without the Word, the Body of Christ cannot be nourished. We are given the responsibility of feeding the Lord's flock. We give a baby believer the milk of the Word, and when he matures he becomes ready for something more solid.

Nourishment for the Believer

As we mature we must continually tend to our own nourishment. Digesting the Word of God is our individual responsibility because we cannot draw all of our spiritual sustenance from church services. Jesus says in John 14:26 that the Holy Spirit will teach us all things. This promise should encourage all of us to devour the Word of God, knowing the Spirit will give us a deeper understanding. As we feed ourselves and in turn feed others, the body of Christ will grow.

Because of Lucifer's deceit in the Garden, God curses him in Genesis 3:14 saying, "Upon thy belly shalt thou go, and dust shalt thou eat all the days of thy life." When we read about Lucifer at the end of the New Testament in Revelation, he has enlarged into a great dragon. This growth is due to his feeding upon the dust, which is the same as flesh since God formed man from the "dust of the ground."

Satan's increase from devouring flesh conveys the idea that our feeding upon fleshly acts will enlarge the kingdom of darkness. For example, whenever we are drawn into gossip, we are increasing the devil's kingdom. On the other hand, edifying people in a Bible study or sharing our testimony with a friend will feed the body of Christ and enlarge the kingdom of God.

We must come to church prepared to worship, arriving with expectations both to receive truths from God and to build up others. Church services should actually be an extension of our holy walk during the week. Healings and blessings need not be postponed for an altar call on Sundays. We should have testimonies of miracles taking place *between* our prayer meetings.

Leesa and I deliberately create worship in our home, gathering together with our children to pray and to encourage each other. There is usually a moment during these times that we recognize God's presence in our midst. It may be through a song, a prayer, or silent reflection. These are precious periods for sharing in which I don't do all the talking. I listen. I want to hear what the

Lord is saying to my wife and children. This foundation prepares us to face our individual trials. It cultivates the idea of sharing each other's burdens and victories, and demonstrates the need to depend upon the Lord for protection and guidance.

Sometimes people avoid such intimate encounters, even with the members of their own family. For whatever reason, people have grown independent of others. They may have experienced an unhealthy codependency and they now reject what can be healthy relationships. Some may have had unhealthy relationships in church, where the ministry was too dependent on the people and the people were too dependent on the ministry. In some instances a trust and control battle ensues. Some ministry leaders are so controlling that they fear if their congregation meets in small groups they will get the wild idea to start their own church. Those who don't trust the Lord and who try to take ownership of others are displaying the orphan mentality.

The Lord can break down the barriers between us. He knows us intimately and can dispel all emotional baggage which prevents us from uniting as the Body of Christ. From here we can effectively reach the world.

Matthew 28:19-20 charges us to, "Go ye therefore, and teach all nations, baptizing them in the name of the Father, and of the Son, and of the Holy Ghost: Teaching them to observe all things whatsoever I have commanded you: and, lo, I am with you alway, even unto the end of the world." It is clear from this passage that fellowshiping and encouraging one another is for the specific purpose of making disciples. We are to invest into others for the continuing expansion of the kingdom of heaven here on earth.

PART IV

WHAT IS MY PURPOSE?

WATCHING ME CHANGE

I began facing the consequences for my wrongdoing at the bank. The whole process lasted two years from the civil lawsuit until my sentencing in May 1999.

During this same period my walk with Christ was thriving. My relationship with Leesa and our children was better than it had ever been. Without realizing it, I was becoming a more loving, attentive husband and father. God was giving me opportunities to minister His Word to people at church and to customers passing through my store.

By June 1999 the time came for me to begin serving my twelve-month prison sentence. Leesa and I spent a lot of time just holding each other and crying. All my children were able to understand was that their father had done something wrong and had to be away for awhile. I took comfort in knowing they had the best mother to care for them in my absence. What especially helped me was the strength of my wife's character. As difficult as it was for us to face the penalty for my wrong, she agreed with me that we had to accept it without complaints. She knew the Lord was still with us through it all.

I sold the store, and Don helped me clean up to make way for the new owner. On my last day I couldn't help but think back, remembering how Don had first come through the front door just two years earlier.

His friendship had changed my life. He showed me the significance of the story about Jesus washing the disciples' feet. When Peter resists receiving this act of servitude, the Lord tells him that he'll have no part with Him if he refuses. Although Don never got around to expounding on this passage, all of his teaching had taught me the meaning of it, how I must allow Jesus to serve me before I can serve Him. We love the Lord only because He first loved us. This is grace. Once I allowed the Lord to reveal Himself and minister to me, I was then able to minister to others. This transformed my view of God and people and even money. The more I learned of the Lord, the more I loved Him. I began understanding even how He viewed me as His child, loving me with abounding love and tenderness.

Don helped carry boxes to my car. The day was warm and we stood awhile outside talking. I told him imprisonment was the consequence for my sin, but I knew God would turn it all in a direction for His purpose.

"The Lord has brought me too far to just let the bottom drop out," I said.

"That's right," he said. "The Lord is taking you on an

assignment down there." He smiled as he talked about God's hand on me. "I'll be here when you come back."

We hugged each other and cried together.

Don took off his glasses and wiped his eyes. "I'll write you, son."

I sat in my car and watched my dear friend get into his old red Buick and drive away.

Don kept his word and wrote me. A letter from him arrived every two weeks. The handwriting was messy and the sentences slanted too far up or too far down the page, but those notes were priceless. I could hear Don's voice in each of them as he encouraged me to look to the end of my imprisonment when I would be reunited with my family.

I answered each letter, writing him about all that was happening in prison.

For the first three months I worked in the kitchen washing dishes. I was glad to fill the days doing something productive. Working with my hands also allowed me to reflect upon the Scriptures I had memorized during the past couple of years. I continued poring over the Bible in my spare time, and I took every opportunity to share Christ with anyone who would listen.

I joined some of the Christian inmates who were having Bible studies. I could feel the hand of God on this group of men as we drew closer in the Lord. More men visited our gatherings and accepted Christ into their lives.

One man who came to our meetings was only twenty-four years old and serving four years for selling drugs. His brother had been killed in a drug deal, and it seemed he was heading down the same dark road. He first came to our Bible studies out of curiosity, but eventually committed his life to the Lord. Thereafter, he was always with me, asking questions, hungry to know more of God. I thought of Don's tender ways of mentoring me as I ministered to this young man.

After my third month in prison, the warden moved me into his office to be his orderly. I filed papers, cleaned the floors, and emptied the trash, performing all my duties to the best of my ability as doing it for the Lord. During this same time I was asked to serve with the chaplain on the prison's Religion Service Council.

The most precious letters came from my wife. I cherished every familiar phrase or word that reflected her sweetness. Every Saturday she would arrive with our two girls. The time for visiting was limited, but I treasured every minute. I longed for the day that I would be reunited with my family.

That day came unexpectedly four months before the completion of my twelve-month sentence. I was called into the warden's office and told to prepare to go home. When I asked why I was being released, the administrative secretary said she didn't know.

I called Leesa and said, "Come get me. I'm coming home."

"And God said, Let us make man in our image, after our likeness: and let them have dominion over the fish of the sea, and over the fowl of the air, and over the cattle, and over all the earth, and over every creeping thing that creepeth upon the earth."

Genesis 1:26

Chapter Eight

Know that You
Are Given Authority

God's Ambassador

Sometimes we might feel like victims of our troubles. With the unending problems and struggles this life brings, it is easy to feel as helpless as a feather tossed about in the wind. However, this perspective is not true. Jesus intends for us to have dominion over our circumstances. As believers in Christ under God's authority, we are not to see ourselves as victims.

Jesus is the King of heaven, residing at the right hand of God and governing everything by His eternal principles. Every aspect and detail of this reign is under His complete authority.

The earth is given to us to establish what is already ordained in heavenly places. Jesus shows us in Matthew 6:10 that we are to pray that God's will be accomplished on this earth as it is in heaven. Equipped by the Lord, we are to establish this heavenly government with all its principles here on earth. The Spirit empowers us so we can tread on every evil that comes against us.

As ambassadors of heaven, we are to plant the kingdom of

heaven everywhere we step. Our entire domain is to be subject to this dominion. The third chapter of Joshua gives a vibrant example of God's authority released through His people. When the priests carry the ark of the Lord across the Jordan, the water instantly retreats from where they step. The river resumes its flow only after the whole nation of Israel crosses to the other side.

God wants to multiply His kingdom through us by releasing His authority everywhere we pass. It is His plan and desire for us to bear much fruit and have control over our circumstances. Once we recognize that God has called us to have dominion on earth, we will no longer feel like a victim. We will understand that every aspect of our life is to be in submission to our spiritual authority. This includes our business, our finances, our health and so much more. We are intended to rule these areas and not let them rule us.

Problems won't disappear, but they will no longer have the power to influence us as they once did. Trouble won't terrify us with its threatening face because we know who we are in Christ: an ambassador of the heavenly kingdom here on this earth. Instead of feeling victimized by problems, we will stand on the Word of God. We realize we don't need to be crying out, "Where are you, God?" because we know where He reigns and how He has given us dominion.

Such as I Have

When Peter walked up to the gate of the temple called Beautiful in Acts 3:6, he told the lame man, "Silver and gold have I none; but such as I have give I thee."

What is it that Peter had that he was able to give the man?

It was obviously more than healing. Clearly, he took the man by the hand and he *was* healed. The beggar's ankles and feet were strengthened, and he leaped about, praising God (Acts 3:7-8). However, Peter was referring to more than giving a new pair of legs. When he proclaimed in the name of Jesus Christ of Nazareth for the man to rise and walk, he was taking dominion over what bound the man. He took authority over what had held him hostage.

Peter understood his authority and claimed it. Too many Christians today might have responded differently to the lame man. They may have carried the beggar into the temple hoping to find someone else to pray over him. Instead of taking dominion over the situation, it might feel safer to just relinquish the responsibility to someone else more spiritual.

Peter was no more of an ambassador of the kingdom of heaven than you or me. If he understood his authority and walked in it, we can too.

Walking and Possessing

We should be walking on earth with dominion, and everywhere the soles of our feet touch, we should generate influence. When we say, "Go!" the devil should retreat in fear. When we say, "Be healed!" to the lame, they should dance on new legs.

Why don't we have these results when God tells us we're supposed to have dominion on this earth? It is because of our double-mindedness. We refuse to proclaim our authority. Instead, we ignore the biblical command for us to act and then place the responsibility on God.

God has purposely limited His power to what we choose to release. He has tied His own hands, so to speak, by equipping us with everything we need to take dominion over all circumstances. When Jesus said it was finished, He appropriated the blood. If we are holy, he has appropriated the blood to our life. We then are also quickened. When He said, "Receive ye the Holy Ghost" (John 20:22), He gave us the same breath of God. With the Holy Spirit connecting us to our heavenly King, we have His heavenly gifts available to us here on earth.

Instead of looking to Jesus as our source of power, we have turned to the false security of religious systems. We have been oppressed by a form of godliness which is lifeless. When the world looks to us for the manifestation of God's authority, they only see dead works.

In Romans 8:19, Paul talks about creation longing for the manifestation of the sons of God. Why is the world waiting for the children of God except for the fact that the Lord wants to intervene through us? The world is victimized by the circumstances of life, and they are longing for an answer. We as believers are to bring them the Good News. This is why Jesus says in John 17:15 that He will not pray for God to take believers out of this world.

God intends for us to have dominion now on earth. He doesn't want our lives placed on hold by thinking the fullness of His blessings only come after we die and go to heaven. We must quit thinking that a new life begins only after death. New life begins now. The power of God is released through us to accomplish His purposes here on earth.

Many people come to church and see manifestation of the

kingdom of God, but they never enter into it. They never claim authority over their own circumstances. If the modern church continues in the same pattern, they will remain in darkness. Complacency has in many cases hardened our hearts toward sin to the point where we are not offended by what offends our God. We don't agonize over the entanglements which destroy the lives of our brothers and sisters in Christ. It is no wonder that we don't experience the power of the kingdom because church has become a lifeless façade of godliness.

Guarding Against Emotionalism

If the government of heaven were really the government here on earth, we would gather together on a Sunday to receive a decree from the King of kings and then go out into the world to establish it. And so, the kingdom of heaven would expand everywhere we went. Why does it have to be any more difficult than this?

What we have done is cheapen the environment in the church by promoting emotionalism and feelings as the foundation of our services. If we don't sell out to sales tactics or market it just right, we fear no one will come. Every time someone is offended, we chase after them to apologize and to soften their hurt. The truth of the matter is Jesus said that offenses are inevitable. Coddling immaturity produces bondage, but communicating the truth will set people free.

We have gotten into a practice of preaching sermons which are generic enough to give nuggets of truth without offending anyone. On the other hand, we direct our strong words of condemnation toward sinners who only know darkness. This approach is backwards. We should be expressing compassion toward those dead in sin, while at the same time, challenging believers to break from dry religiosity.

This change begins with challenging the church's leadership. I thank God for pastors who lead the charge, who stand up and point their fingers to the truth.

As a church, we are living less than effective lives, but this can be turned around. Once we recognize that we are in the world but not of the world, everything changes. We will then operate by the principles of Scripture. We will be guided by the Spirit of God and not by our own limited power and authority.

Understanding Mind-sets

Everyone is limited to their own mind-set. We each speak and act according to our individual perspective whether we realize it or not. Those who are under our authority whether at work or in our family, know how we think based on what we have said and done. Accordingly, they model their own behavior and restrain some of their actions due to our expectations.

For example, if my wife wants to buy a five-hundred-dollar purse, she would already know my response before she even asked. She is going to make a decision based on how she knows I think. She is restrained because she already knows my mind-set. My children who are in submission to me as their father also know my values on spending and will act accordingly.

I could even say to my wife that it was okay to buy the purse, but she wouldn't feel comfortable because she knew how

I really felt about it. On the other hand, if I proved to her with my words that I wanted her to have the purse, she would suddenly understand I had a change of mind-set. Then she could purchase it without feeling guilty. She is now going to operate under a different understanding. The principalities, so to speak, that once had a stronghold on her are broken. She can now walk in a new freedom.

This is similar to how we can walk in new freedom once our mind-set changes to understanding God's abounding love for us.

Religiosity Uncovered

Sincerity and openness will draw people to Christ. When we put up a front and pretend not to have personal struggles, we appear as frauds to the watching world. Those seeking an answer don't expect to find it from perfect people. In fact, they are more apt to believe those who have overcome similar problems as their own.

Many of us have difficulty winning our families to the Lord because we don't interact with our families as we should. We manifest pride, trying to prove to them that we have all the answers. God does not call us to act like we are better than others. Our lives should be an invitation for others to see what we have learned of God. Exhibiting selfless love is a powerful way to reach our family.

Upon this Rock

When Jesus asked His disciples who they said He was, Simon Peter answered in Matthew 16:16 that He was the Christ, the Son of the living God. The Lord then told him that His Father in heaven had revealed this to him. "And I say also unto thee," the Lord continued, "that thou art Peter, and upon this rock I will build my church."

This rock refers to the heavenly kingdom described in Daniel 2:44-45 which will destroy all other kingdoms. It is the stone that is "cut out of the mountain without hands." This passage in Daniel emphasizes that there is only one true kingdom, namely the kingdom of heaven which Christ came to establish. So eternal is this kingdom that Jesus said that not even the gates of hell shall prevail against it.

All for a Divine Purpose

Christ's death on a cross, the shedding of His blood, His resurrection, His many healings and miracles, all were a means to a divine end. The purpose of all this was to initiate the rule of His kingdom. Jesus restored dominion to the children of God because it was His plan since the beginning of time. Adam chose independence, but the only begotten Son, Jesus Christ Himself, came to reconcile man to God. Only through this reconciliation would man be able to establish the kingdom of God on earth.

We don't have to learn all the rules and regulations of God's kingdom. We only need to recognize our heavenly citizenship, because He has freely given to His children the ability to reign over all the earth.

The Scriptures declare the independence that Jesus has given us. At the moment of salvation, we immediately forsake the kingdom of darkness for the kingdom of light. We don't have to live by the world's dark system any longer. The elements of earth and all of our circumstances are subject to us. Even our body which comes from the earth is subject to our dominion.

When we got saved we received the Spirit of God that allows us to see and enter into all that God has for us. Now we have to learn the truths of the Bible. We have to understand this declaration of the heavenly kingdom so we may operate effectively.

Living out God's divine plan means more than simply going to church and mouthing half-hearted prayers. This new life is radical because it goes against the grain of our modern culture. Walking with our Creator is at the core of it. As we mature spiritually we will understand that our praying is actually petitioning our heavenly Father.

God is now raising up people in this generation who are no longer satisfied with the status quo. I am seeing more and more people yearning for an intimate relationship with the Majesty on high. The season has arrived for us to see the establishment of His kingdom through the lives of His faithful servants.

"And it shall come to pass, if thou shalt hearken diligently unto the voice of the Lord thy God, to observe and to do all his commandments which I command thee this day, that the Lord thy God will set thee on high above all nations of the earth."

Deuteronomy 28:1

Chapter Nine

CHANGE HAPPENS

Seasons of Life

Would Have! Could Have! Should Have! These three phrases express the regrets felt by most people. "My life would have been better," we think, "if I had only taken a different course or stayed where I was or met someone else or lived in a different place."

We walk through life from beginning to end making choices. It would be impossible for every decision we make to always be the best. Everyone has regrets of some sort.

Life is comprised of seasons, from birth to death. Some periods come and go with certain predictability like spring following winter. Other seasons surprise us with a blustery storm instead of the anticipated balmy day. There are horrendous times in which we hang on with white knuckles, praying the season will end. We have all been there. Sometimes we exhaust ourselves just trying to figure out the season in which we find ourselves.

Whether we acknowledge it or not, all of us are in some kind of season. No matter what the circumstances are during this period of time, we need to recognize that God can accomplish great things through us. We must understand our season and allow God to finish His perfect work in us. Our past is forever gone, and what's ahead is yet for us to face. We need to only concern ourselves with the season of today.

A Season and a Purpose

Ecclesiastes 3:1 tells us, "To every thing there is a season, and a time to every purpose under the heaven." This Scripture states clearly that nothing is separate from the plan of God. Every situation, every trouble, every experience all have a purpose in our lives. We know from other passages in the Bible that the Lord does not allow challenges in our lives except those He can work to our growth and benefit.

We must know that God can redeem our situations, our days, our lives. Nothing passes in our life as insignificant. God establishes purpose and meaning to every area for His kingdom and for our good. No matter what happens, He uses it to bring us further into the person He wants us to be. We are more transformed into the likeness of Christ after struggling through our trials because God is constantly shaping us.

Ecclesiastes 3:9 asks what profit is there for those toiling in their work. The second half of verse 10 answers the question with the phrase, "God hath given to the sons of men to be exercised in it." Just like physical exercise, the many seasons of our life build us up to become stronger and more capable. Both through hard times and good times, we can exercise and develop our faith.

I often think of life as a series of time frames. There is a point in time when we are conceived and born, and there is a point in time in which we die. Within the short span of these years are a number of time frames or sequences, each punctuated with milestones. We can sometimes divide these periods based on graduating from high school or getting married or having children or beginning a career.

We need to enjoy the season in which we find ourselves. There is plenty of time to move into the next season so we need to appreciate the unique aspects of the present one. Too many times we miss out on blessings because we only focus on immediate hardships and yearn for an escape into an easier period.

For example, raising children is a blessed season but not an easy one. This period of teddy bears and high chairs awes us with the introduction of our new baby. We can't help but want to hold him or her, thrilled over their giggle or the way they grip our finger. We just can't get over such a miracle. With this wondrous blessing, difficulty arrives. Just as we sink into a restful sleep, the cries of a fussy baby wake us up to his particular feeding schedule. Working all day and having to rise early the next day is no matter to him. This little fellow is on his own time schedule. Diaper changing begins feeling like an hourly event.

If we only spend our moments dreaming of escape, we can miss the wondrous moments which will remain dear to our hearts for the rest of our days. Frustration comes when we desire the season of having children but resent the elements that accompany it. Babies bring change into our lives, and it cannot all be pleasant. We must embrace it as a season of blessing and opportunity to grow in knowledge and patience. If we don't, we may find ourselves years later longing for what has already passed.

God has a purpose for us within each time frame. The

reason, for example, of the courting stage of a relationship is to get to know our future spouse. If we impatiently only think about the next stage, we miss what we should have gained. We may find ourselves in the marriage season wedded to someone we don't even know. The period of courtship is to bring benefits to a couple and to equip them for a lifelong relationship. It can also be a warning period in which the couple learns they shouldn't marry at all.

As we move on to the next season of life, we must not look backward and try recouping what has been lost in the previous period. Regrets drive us in this direction, expressing itself in the wasted reflections of "if I had only." Nothing is more tragic than realizing at the end of life that we have wasted years mulling over past mistakes. When we dwell on the past we miss the purpose for the time that we are in now.

We cannot always control when the season changes. Sometimes a job loss or a doctor's report or a spouse filing for divorce abruptly changes the period of time without notice. There are moments when the whole season seems ambushed by impossible circumstances, propelling us into an unknown direction.

Recognize the Season

Most of the time, however, the change of seasons is as predictable as summer moving into fall. This progression could even be compared to the sequences of a day. The morning of our life usually entails living at home with our parents and going to school, while the late afternoon will most likely find us paying a mortgage and raising children.

Understanding the present season is vital for gaining the most benefits. Not being cognizant of our particular time frame inhibits our ability to meet the demands of the moment. This kind of spiritual blindness is like wearing tank tops in the winter or heavy coats in the summer. Someone, for example, may simultaneously be in a season of both raising their children and building a career. Neglecting either responsibility would create loss. They need to build a financial future to provide for the family, but not to the extent of neglecting their children. Spending all their time with work will rob them of precious moments with their loved ones. When the children are grown and the relationship with them is empty, this person can only feel loss.

Knowing which season we are in and acting accordingly maximizes our lives. It allows us to minimize regret in the future and keeps us from wasting precious hours agonizing over the past. Overcoming bad decisions with good ones only comes from recognizing the present period of time.

Not all seasons are fruitful in the sense of acquiring something like a college degree or developing a relationship for marriage. However, they are productive as a period of reflection and fostering a new mind-set. This season may feel barren and cold like winter, but it can reap vast dividends. The slow pace and isolation of this occasion opens up more time for prayer and seeking God's direction. This can be a time for pruning bad habits and entanglements out of our life.

We must recognize that we aren't the only ones who experience these periods. Others suffer through these times too.

Frequently people believe that the cause for these dry spells is sin in their lives. Self-examination and repentance may be a good place to start, but this isn't necessarily the reason for these times. God may have a particular purpose during this period which was never brought in our lives due to sin. A season of isolation and quiet rather than a period of incessant busyness might be the only environment in which we can gain a particular truth from the Lord.

We should never take it up on ourselves to tell someone that sin has caused their barren season. Instead, we should just help them find out what God is trying to teach them. If sin is the cause for their harsh period, then they will learn this as they seek the Lord.

The Lord, who has started His work in us, will finish it. He will perfect His plans for us even through the dry spells. Growth during this time may not be as visible as during other times, but it can be life-changing. We must be obedient to the Lord as we follow His leading, and He will bring the growth.

Seasons Change

A season is not forever; it is for a designated period. God wants us to recognize each time frame so we can realize when we must move on. Camping too long in any season will inhibit our growth and cut us off from the blessings of the next season.

For example, I know people who have adapted their lives around an illness that has plagued them for years. After receiving healing they continue living as though they are still sick. The disease is more familiar to them than the newly restored health. They choose to live out the rest of their days just as they did when they were ill. God moved them on to a much better period of life but they remain in the last season of heartache.

Parents who refuse to accept their children as grown, capable adults are no different. They continue treating them as if they are still young and living at home. This behavior prevents their moving into the next season, and it sometimes keeps their adult children dependent in an unhealthy way. This often fosters resentment toward the parents.

In my own life I have noticed that with each season change I either gain or lose a relationship. God lessens my interaction with someone, or He brings a new person into my life.

During a change of seasons we may gain or lose something significant. Perhaps it is contact vital for the growth of our business. Maybe the company has operated in the same way for several years with much success and then suddenly, factors outside of our control cause change. An ongoing contract which had provided stability for the business is now ended. Something like this is a good sign that the season is changing.

Our initial response is to hang onto what is familiar and try to continue as we have always done. The process worked in the past so we feel safer with it. Instead, we need to readjust our thinking so we can recognize the new doors which are opening.

Mary's New Season

Mary was invited into a new season when the angel Gabriel announced that she was going to give birth to Jesus, the Son of the Most High (Luke 1:26-38). She had no right to God during these days except through a high priest. Yet, God chose her. Mary didn't create this plan and then bring it to the Father. Instead, God designed His plan for restoring humanity back into His fellowship, and He brought this good news to Mary.

In the same way, God initiated our salvation. He drew us to Him. We heard the Word of God and made a conscious effort to open our heart to Him, receiving redemption by faith. We didn't even know how to cry out to God or gain access to Him. All we knew was our life needed change. Then someone in some way, whether in person or by something written, reached us. The Word of God came to us and, like Mary, we recognized that God was initiating something. When we received His Word, Jesus took up residence within us.

Mary had no concept of what was about to take place. She only knew what had been revealed by the angel. The Holy Spirit was going to overshadow her and place something inside of her. This is what happens when we are saved. When we give our heart to the Lord, the Holy Spirit overshadows us and places a design of God's life inside us. Our mission then is to allow it to be fulfilled in our lifetime. Anything short of this will not accomplish God's plan for you and me.

It is our responsibility to commit our ways to the Lord to fulfill God's purpose in our life, but it is God who initiates salvation from the very beginning. He knows our need and meets it. Through our spiritual growth we take more control of what God has started. At the same time, the Lord directs our steps and finishes His work in us. Our biggest struggle is trying to force outcomes rather than allowing God to complete His work through us.

Our Responsibility

Mary conceived a child by the power of the Holy Spirit at God's appointed time. Her responsibility upon hearing God's plan was to believe and receive it. With the birth of Jesus, Mary entered into a new season for her to nurture and raise her child. Through the course of this journey she had to rely upon God for direction to make right decisions.

We have the same responsibility to understand what the Word of God says, and then we must allow God to complete His work through us. It is not our responsibility to make His plan come to pass. If we don't want to miss all God has intended for us, we must learn that He said He will finish the work. When we try to bring everything to pass in our own efforts, we short-circuit God's power through us. If we didn't have any part in our salvation, how do we think it's our responsibility to accomplish the Lord's plan? Our job is to be patient and follow the Word of God.

Mary had a relationship with Jesus the full thirty-three years of His life. She knew He was the Savior but He was also her son. When time arrived for His crucifixion, she had to let Him go. How many of us would have tried to interfere with His prophesied humiliation and death? We might have argued He was too young to die or He could do more for the world if He were spared.

Jesus knew His purpose and faced it willingly. Mary was able to accept the fate of her child because she knew His reason for coming into this world. She knew her purpose was to give birth to the Savior. After investing her life into Him, she knew not to interfere with God's plan no matter how horrific the consequences were for her son. Both Jesus and Mary understood the direction of

God and cooperated with His plan.

God has a plan and a purpose for you and me. If God has called us to something, then He will accomplish it. We should rejoice that the Lord has spoken to us and His Spirit has overshadowed us. We must foster our desire to fulfill this purpose and allow it to solidify as a vision in our heart and mind. When we let the Lord confirm this plan by showing what He will do in and through us, no one can deter us from God's direction.

All for God's Glory

Mary didn't persuade God to make her Jesus' mother. God chose Mary. It wasn't even her responsibility to figure out how the plan of redemption was to unfold. She simply remained faithful and God carried out His purpose through Jesus.

Sometimes in our attempt to gain self-worth, we want to know every detail of God's plan for us. We want to feel important, that God is using us in a grand way. Rather than being satisfied knowing that the Lord is active in our lives, we want to take ownership of the process. This is not the same as desiring a deeper understanding so that we may serve the Lord more effectively. Instead, it is a prideful pursuit as we assign more value to people hearing about our Christian walk than we assign to the wonder of participating in it.

We battle for the glory that belongs only to God. It's tempting to feel self-important when God brings us victory or raises our position. When we start thinking triumph comes through our own efforts, we will impede the Lord's work in our lives. The abundant life only comes when we allow the Lord to overshadow us.

What if you were Joseph whose purpose was being the husband of Mary? The writings about him in the Bible are minimal. Today we would expect Joseph to receive a lot of fame and financial benefits. We would anticipate a bestselling book or blockbuster movie to depict his story. He should at least, we think, be the pastor of a mega church. Without such public affirmation we would be convinced he was missing his purpose. However, the truth is Joseph humbly remained faithful to his calling, and after two thousand years people still marvel at his life.

Transformation with Each Season

Our challenge is to allow God to start and finish His work in us. The journey from beginning to end is comprised of time frames and seasons. We are in the lives of people for a while, and then we are out of their lives. We hold positions of work for a period, and this also changes. We watch the transformation of our children from infants to toddlers to teenagers to young adults.

Each new season should bring about personal change. If we parent our adult child as we did when he was a teenager, then we don't understand the demands of the present season. If we operate on our job in the fifteenth year as we did in the first, we aren't growing with our experience.

When God opens a door we must walk through it and when He closes it we must look for the new direction. A closed door doesn't mean we've done something wrong. It is simply a sign that God is changing the season. If our company starts failing it doesn't prove that we're a bad business owner, but simply that God is changing the season of our life.

The beginning of Ecclesiastes tells us there is a time to plant and a time to uproot, a time to weep and a time to laugh, a time to keep and a time to cast away. God sent His angel to Mary at His appointed hour. We don't have to spend a lifetime searching to recognize our designated times. If we will just lift up our eyes and recognize what the Lord has brought us, then we will see the nature of the season.

If we understand we are supposed to deal with the issues of the moment, it will help us move past that season into the next season. When it appears that the bottom has fallen out, it could very well mean our season has changed. Instead of trying to go back and do as we have always done, we should regard our situation differently. If we've made some bad decisions, we need to acknowledge it and let the season go. Then we should agree to let God accomplish His purpose in us as we enter the next season with our eyes wide open.

Some Christians have had a marriage that went bad and subsequently went through divorce. The season of that marriage is finished and behind them. God can take this or any bad situation and turn their life around for the better. In this case they need to be careful not to bring the old season into the new marriage. If they invest their lingering hurt and anger into the new relationship, it will spoil the blessings in the present season. If they act the same as they did in the previous relationship, then the marriage in the new season won't be any different than the marriage in the old one.

Your Steps Are Ordered

When God opens a door for us it's usually through a

relationship with a person. Often, it is someone whom we didn't know in the last season. These friendships need to be authentic and caring. If we hold others at a distance, we may never cultivate the relationship through which God wants to bless us. If our steps are being ordered by the Lord, then He is bringing these people across our path in order to usher us into the new season.

Sometimes the relationship that God uses to change us is uncomfortable. He may send someone who is dependent and needy who frustrates and drains us. Yet, the Lord burdens our heart to help them. We may reach out to someone who resists our help and even angers us, but we just cannot turn our back on them. When God brings people into our lives to teach us or to open a door it may not always be a typical relationship. Yet, it pushes us in a definite direction and initiates a new season. It may also open a new period for the other person as well.

There's nothing wrong with asking God to clarify His reason for bringing a new person into our life. We may ask Him, "Why are we together?" or "What am I to learn in this relationship?" or "How am I to help this person?"

It is worthy to ask God to help us understand our present season. The more we know about His purpose and direction, the less we will resist His will. Without this kind of wisdom we will waste our energy and time chasing after what is frivolous and separate from God.

Whenever we feel prideful about God using us we must remember that everything is to be done for the glory of the Lord. God doesn't need us to start or finish His work. He could easily choose another believer. Instead of puffing ourselves up with pride, we should be thankful for the privilege of participating in His divine purposes.

"But the anointing which ye have received of him abideth in you, and ye need not that any man teach you, but as the same anointing teacheth you of all things, and is truth, and is no lie, and even as it hath taught you, ye shall abide in him."

1 John 2:27

Chapter Ten

KNOW THE PURPOSE OF GOD'S ANOINTING UPON YOUR LIFE

Purpose of God's Anointing

Jesus restored the broken-hearted, freed the captive, and healed the sick during His ministry. As His followers, we too must carry on His work. The reason the Lord anoints us through His Spirit is for us to carry on His mission. All is for the purpose of Jesus establishing the kingdom of heaven through us.

If we want to receive the Lord's blessings we must cooperate with Him, submitting to His authority and direction. Jesus illustrated this kind of commitment to His father, remaining faithful all the way to His own death. He was humble, yet strong. There is no record of Him exhibiting pride or arrogance. This very fact should prove the importance of humility. When we think we know everything, we are no longer teachable, and our spiritual growth is hindered.

Listening exhibits a teachable spirit and is more beneficial than talking. We all have a reservoir of information within us, and we increase our knowledge by listening. I have personally discovered the need to talk less and listen more. Growth in this way is for the purpose of helping others in their time of need.

The Anointing of Jesus

Jesus began His life in obscurity. Then at the appointed time, He was publicly affirmed by the Father. This happened after He was baptized by John and the Spirit of God descended upon Him, anointing Him in preparation for His ministry.

At that moment everything changed. Jesus left His season of preparation for a new season of ministry. His authority was established with the anointing of the Holy Spirit. He didn't speak like the scribes or Pharisees or anybody else. Every word He spoke rang out in truth and with authority. People knew Jesus was anointed by the power of His words.

People take notice of those who are anointed of God. It is obvious to the world that their lives are extraordinary. The Spirit of God accomplishes through them what cannot be achieved through ordinary means.

Jesus walked all His life among sick and spiritually-enslaved people, but He never healed them until after His anointing and the start of His ministry. Sometimes this is the same for us. We walk in obscurity, and then God anoints us for His divine purpose. After we mature into spiritual fathers and mothers, we begin helping and teaching others.

We are Anointed by God

God's children today have carried a slavery mind-set for too long. The Lord wants us to understand that we are anointed by Him. This power is not given to us for our selfish gain, but should pass through our lives to bless others. Only then will we see the hand of God manifested in our lives.

The tragic truth is most Christians never experience this kind of intimate relationship with the Lord. Many hear the words of Jesus but they never understand their meaning. Too many believers live out each day of their lives without ever understanding the fullness of what Jesus came to bring them. Their lack of awareness is similar to the ignorance of unbelievers who, according to Mark 4:12, hear and don't understand.

His Word in Our Hearts

Holding the Word of God in our head is important but insufficient. At that point it is only an idea or philosophical thought. It can easily be stolen by the enemy before it takes root in our heart. Someone with another perspective could present a more convincing argument and persuade us in their direction. However, if God's Word reaches down into our spirit, to the very core of who we are, then nobody can take it away from us. The Truth of God must move from our head and into our heart. Sometimes we want to gain intimacy with the Lord with an easy, quick fix. Rather than spending time praying and meditating upon the Scriptures, we hope to gain God's influence by the laying on of hands.

To prevent the enemy from stealing God's Word from us, we must allow His promises to become part of us. While in the wilderness of Judah with enemies seeking his life, David wrote in Psalm 63:6, "I remember thee upon my bed, and meditate on thee in the night watches." He knew especially during the difficult times that victory comes when God's precepts and promises are implanted into our hearts. Intimacy with our Lord results from us allowing His truth to grow in the very fabric of our being.

As we mature in Christ we will recognize that everything works together for our good. Even suffering benefits us, shaping our character and making us stronger. As Christ forms in us, we will minister to others and impart God's truth into their lives. This comes from His word being inside of us. If His truths are only in our head, then we cannot impart them into someone else's heart.

As we allow God to draw us into a deeper faith, then we will automatically transfer light and truth to others. We can comfort and encourage those who are hurting. Through the power of the Holy Spirit we can minister life to our family and to people in our workplace. Everywhere we go we can bring the hope of Christ.

Jesus in Us, the Hope of Glory

Colossians 1:26-27 explains the wondrous unveiling of God's plan for mankind, saying, "even the mystery which hath been hid from ages and from generations, but now is made manifest to his saints: to whom God would make known what is the riches of the glory of this mystery among the Gentiles; which is Christ in you, the hope of glory."

Jesus reached out to the poor and the broken-hearted people of this world. He brought comfort and restoration to those in need. He didn't come for Himself but for us. In the same way, our hope through Christ is not just for our benefit. We are to minister the same life and light to others.

Maybe the Lord has given you a vision or promise which has not yet come to pass. Problems or entanglements may have discouraged you in your walk. The glorious news is Christ is always stretching out his arms for you to run to Him. You may feel captive but God's deliverance for you is now. We all must forget the mistakes and sins of yesterday and chase after God who loves us as His children.

The kingdom of heaven is at hand, and it is here in our midst. An abundant and victorious life is ours. With Jesus, the hope of glory in us, we can establish His kingdom right here on earth and reach those hearts hungering for a Savior.

HEARING FROM MY FRIEND

After being released from prison, I became more involved with Christ Temple Church in Huntington, West Virginia. In February 2000 I became the ministerial team leader. I got together with Don only a few times during this period, but we talked by phone several times a week.

Don's health was failing. He was coughing more and his voice was becoming weaker. He was still living in the high-rise and involved with the residents. He had also begun staying with his daughter in Columbus, Ohio at different intervals.

In 2002 I began serving as the executive pastor and my schedule became much busier. However, I continued my phone calls with Don.

About a year later I was interviewed on a local Christian TV broadcast. I discussed how the Word of God pointed the way to Christ. "Jesus," I told the host, "is revealed from cover to cover, from Genesis to Revelation." The passages which I quoted as proof were the very Scriptures Don had taught me and were now a part of me.

As I left the studio and was driving off the parking lot, my cell phone rang. It was Don calling. He told me he was very sick and was planning to move in permanently with his daughter.

I didn't know that this was going to be our last conversation, and I would never be able to reach him again. He was going to pass out of my life as quickly as he had walked into it.

"I watched you on the broadcast, son," Don said. "The student has now become the teacher."

Selected Scripture References

Introduction

Matthew 4:17:

> From that time Jesus began to preach, and to say, Repent: for the kingdom of heaven is at hand.

Luke 4:42-44:

> And when it was day, he departed and went into a desert place: and the people sought him, and came unto him, and stayed him, that he should not depart from them.
>
> And he said unto them, I must preach the kingdom of God to other cities also: for therefore am I sent.
>
> And he preached in the synagogues of Galilee.

Matthew 13:24-30:

> Another parable put he forth unto them, saying, The kingdom of heaven is likened unto a man which sowed good seed in his field:
>
> But while men slept, his enemy came and sowed tares among the wheat, and went his way.
>
> But when the blade was sprung up, and brought forth

fruit, then appeared the tares also.

So the servants of the householder came and said unto him, Sir, didst not thou sow good seed in thy field? from whence then hath it tares?

He said unto them, An enemy hath done this. The servants said unto him, Wilt thou then that we go and gather them up?

But he said, Nay; lest while ye gather up the tares, ye root up also the wheat with them.

Let both grow together until the harvest: and in the time of harvest I will say to the reapers, Gather ye together first the tares, and bind them in bundles to burn them: but gather the wheat into my barn.

Matthew 13:31-32:

Another parable put he forth unto them, saying, The kingdom of heaven is like to a grain of mustard seed, which a man took, and sowed in his field:

Which indeed is the least of all seeds: but when it is grown, it is the greatest among herbs, and becometh a tree, so that the birds of the air come and lodge in the branches thereof.

Matthew 13:33:

> Another parable spake he unto them; The kingdom of
> heaven is like unto leaven, which a woman took, and hid in
> three measures of meal, till the whole was leavened.

Titus 2:13:

> Looking for that blessed hope, and the glorious appearing
> of the great God and our Saviour Jesus Christ.

Psalm 1:3,6:

> And he shall be like a tree planted by the rivers of water,
> that bringeth forth his fruit in his season; his leaf also shall
> not wither; and whatsoever he doeth shall prosper.

> For the Lord knoweth the way of the righteous: but the
> way of the ungodly shall perish.

Matthew 13:44:

> Again, the kingdom of heaven is like unto treasure hid in a
> field; the which when a man hath found, he hideth, and for
> joy thereof goeth and selleth all that he hath, and buyeth
> that field.

Part I — What Did Jesus Mean?

Chapter One
It's Here, It's Now

> *"From that time Jesus began to preach, and to say,*
> *Repent: for the kingdom of heaven is at hand."*
> **Matthew 4:17**

John 10:10:

> The thief cometh not, but for to steal, and to kill, and to
> destroy: I am come that they might have life, and that they
> might have it more abundantly.

2 Corinthians 5:17:

> Therefore if any man be in Christ, he is a new creature: old
> things are passed away; behold, all things are become new.

Matthew 4:17:

> From that time Jesus began to preach, and to say, Repent:
> for the kingdom of heaven is at hand.

Genesis 2:8-20:

> And the Lord God planted a garden eastward in Eden; and
> there he put the man whom he had formed.
>
> And out of the ground made the Lord God to grow every

tree that is pleasant to the sight, and good for food; the tree of life also in the midst of the garden, and the tree of knowledge of good and evil.

And a river went out of Eden to water the garden; and from thence it was parted, and became into four heads.

The name of the first is Pison: that is it which compasseth the whole land of Havilah, where there is gold;

And the gold of that land is good: there is bdellium and the onyx stone.

And the name of the second river is Gihon: the same is it that compasseth the whole land of Ethiopia.

And the name of the third river is Hiddekel: that is it which goeth toward the east of Assyria. And the fourth river is Euphrates.

And the Lord God took the man, and put him into the garden of Eden to dress it and to keep it.

And the Lord God commanded the man, saying, Of every tree of the garden thou mayest freely eat:

But of the tree of the knowledge of good and evil, thou shalt not eat of it: for in the day that thou eatest thereof thou shalt surely die.

And the Lord God said, It is not good that the man should be alone; I will make him a help meet for him.

And out of the ground the Lord God formed every beast of the field, and every fowl of the air; and brought them unto Adam to see what he would call them: and whatsoever Adam called every living creature, that was the name thereof.

And Adam gave names to all cattle, and to the fowl of the air, and to every beast of the field; but for Adam there was not found a help meet for him.

Genesis 1:26:

And God said, Let us make man in our image, after our likeness: and let them have dominion over the fish of the sea, and over the fowl of the air, and over the cattle, and over all the earth, and over every creeping thing that creepeth upon the earth.

Genesis 3:1-10:

Now the serpent was more subtile than any beast of the field which the Lord God had made. And he said unto the woman, Yea, hath God said, Ye shall not eat of every tree of the garden?

And the woman said unto the serpent, We may eat of the fruit of the trees of the garden:

But of the fruit of the tree which is in the midst of the garden, God hath said, Ye shall noteat of it, neither shall ye touch it, lest ye die.

And the serpent said unto the woman, Ye shall not surely die:

For God doth know that in the day ye eat thereof, then your eyes shall be opened, and ye shall be as gods, knowing good and evil.

And when the woman saw that the tree was good for food, and that it was pleasant to the eyes, and a tree to be desired to make one wise, she took of the fruit thereof, and did eat, and gave also unto her husband with her; and he did eat.

And the eyes of them both were opened, and they knew that they were naked; and they sewed fig leaves together, and made themselves aprons.

And they heard the voice of the Lord God walking in the garden in the cool of the day: and Adam and his wife hid themselves from the presence of the Lord God amongst the trees of the garden.

And the Lord God called unto Adam, and said unto him, Where art thou?

And he said, I heard thy voice in the garden, and I was afraid, because I was naked; and I hid myself.

Psalms 115:16:

> The heaven, even the heavens, are the Lord's: but the earth hath he given to the children of men.

Genesis 3:16-19:

> Unto the woman he said, I will greatly multiply thy sorrow and thy conception; in sorrow thou shalt bring forth children; and thy desire shall be to thy husband, and he shall rule over thee.
>
> And unto Adam he said, Because thou hast hearkened unto the voice of thy wife, and hast eaten of the tree, of which I commanded thee, saying, Thou shalt not eat of it: cursed is the ground for thy sake; in sorrow shalt thou eat of it all the days of thy life;
>
> Thorns also and thistles shall it bring forth to thee; and thou shalt eat the herb of the field;
>
> In the sweat of thy face shalt thou eat bread, till thou return unto the ground; for out of it wast thou taken: for dust thou art, and unto dust shalt thou return.

Luke 2:14:

> Glory to God in the highest, and on earth peace, good will toward men.

Acts 23:8:

> For the Sadducees say that there is no resurrection, neither angel, nor spirit: but the Pharisees confess both.

Luke 12:32:

> Fear not, little flock; for it is your Father's good pleasure to give you the kingdom.

John 3:5:

> Jesus answered, Verily, verily, I say unto thee, Except a man be born of water and of the Spirit, he cannot enter into the kingdom of God.

Romans 14:17:

> For the kingdom of God is not meat and drink; but righteousness, and peace, and joy in the Holy Ghost.

Matthew 6:10:

> Thy kingdom come. Thy will be done in earth, as it is in heaven.

Matthew 11:30:

> For my yoke is easy, and my burden is light.

Chapter Two
Mind-sets Matter

"The heavens declare the glory of God;
and the firmament showeth his handiwork."

Psalm 19:1

Matthew 9:17:

> Neither do men put new wine into old bottles: else the bottles break, and the wine runneth out, and the bottles perish: but they put new wine into new bottles, and both are preserved.

Luke 4:4:

> And Jesus answered him, saying, It is written, That man shall not live by bread alone, but by every word of God.

John 14:12:

> Verily, verily, I say unto you, He that believeth on me, the works that I do shall he do also; and greater works than these shall he do; because I go unto my Father.

1 Corinthians 4:15:

> For though ye have ten thousand instructors in Christ, yet have ye not many fathers: for in Christ Jesus I have

begotten you through the gospel.

Acts 19:12:

> So that from his body were brought unto the sick handkerchiefs or aprons, and the diseases departed from them, and the evil spirits went out of them.

Psalm 121:2:

> My help cometh from the Lord, which made heaven and earth.

Romans 12:2:

> And be not conformed to this world: but be ye transformed by the renewing of your mind, that ye may prove what is that good, and acceptable, and perfect will of God.

1 Chronicles 16:24:

> Declare his glory among the heathen; his marvelous works among all nations.

1 Samuel 5:1:

> And the Philistines took the ark of God, and brought it from Ebenezer unto Ashdod.

1 Samuel 6:1-21:

And the ark of the Lord was in the country of the Philistines seven months.

And the Philistines called for the priests and the diviners, saying, What shall we do to the ark of the Lord? tell us wherewith we shall send it to his place.

And they said, If ye send away the ark of the God of Israel, send it not empty; but in any wise return him a trespass offering: then ye shall be healed, and it shall be known to you why his hand is not removed from you.

Then said they, What shall be the trespass offering which we shall return to him? They answered, Five golden emerods, and five golden mice, according to the number of the lords of the Philistines: for one plague was on you all, and on your lords.

Wherefore ye shall make images of your emerods, and images of your mice that mar the land; and ye shall give glory unto the God of Israel: peradventure he will lighten his hand from off you, and from off your gods, and from off your land.

Wherefore then do ye harden your hearts, as the Egyptians and Pharaoh hardened their hearts? when he had wrought wonderfully among them, did they not let the people go, and they departed?

Now therefore make a new cart, and take two milch kine, on which there hath come no yoke, and tie the kine to the cart, and bring their calves home from them:

And take the ark of the Lord, and lay it upon the cart; and put the jewels of gold, which ye return him for a trespass offering, in a coffer by the side thereof; and send it away, that it may go.

And see, if it goeth up by the way of his own coast to Bethshemesh, then he hath done us this great evil: but if not, then we shall know that it is not his hand that smote us: it was a chance that happened to us.

And the men did so; and took two milch kine, and tied them to the cart, and shut up their calves at home:

And they laid the ark of the Lord upon the cart, and the coffer with the mice of gold and the images of their emerods.

And the kine took the straight way to the way of Bethshemesh, and went along the highway, lowing as they went, and turned not aside to the right hand or to the left; and the lords of the Philistines went after them unto the border of Bethshemesh.

And they of Bethshemesh were reaping their wheat harvest in the valley: and they lifted up their eyes, and saw the ark, and rejoiced to see it.

And the cart came into the field of Joshua, a Bethshemite, and stood there, where there was a great stone: and they clave the wood of the cart, and offered the kine a burnt offering unto the Lord.

And the Levites took down the ark of the Lord, and the coffer that was with it, wherein the jewels of gold were, and put them on the great stone: and the men of Bethshemesh offered burnt offerings and sacrificed sacrifices the same day unto the Lord.

And when the five lords of the Philistines had seen it, they returned to Ekron the same day.

And these are the golden emerods which the Philistines returned for a trespass offering unto the Lord; for Ashdod one, for Gaza one, for Askelon one, for Gath one, for Ekron one;

And the golden mice, according to the number of all the cities of the Philistines belonging to the five lords, both of fenced cities, and of country villages, even unto the great stone of Abel, whereon they set down the ark of the Lord: which stone remaineth unto this day in the field of Joshua, the Bethshemite.

And he smote the men of Bethshemesh, because they had looked into the ark of the Lord, even he smote of the people fifty thousand and threescore and ten men: and the people lamented, because the Lord had smitten many of the people with a great slaughter.

And the men of Bethshemesh said, Who is able to stand before this holy Lord God? and to whom shall he go up from us?

And they sent messengers to the inhabitants of Kirjathjearim, saying, The Philistines have brought again the ark of the Lord; come ye down, and fetch it up to you.

1 Samuel 7:1-2:

And the men of Kirjathjearim came, and fetched up the ark of the Lord, and brought it into the house of Abinadab in the hill, and sanctified Eleazar his son to keep the ark of the Lord.

And it came to pass, while the ark abode in Kirjathjearim, that the time was long; for it was twenty years: and all the house of Israel lamented after the Lord.

2 Samuel 6:1-15:

Again, David gathered together all the chosen men of Israel, thirty thousand.

And David arose, and went with all the people that were with him from Baale of Judah, to bring up from thence the ark of God, whose name is called by the name of the Lord of hosts that dwelleth between the cherubim.

And they set the ark of God upon a new cart, and brought it out of the house of Abinadab that was in Gibeah: and Uzzah and Ahio, the sons of Abinadab, drave the new cart.

And they brought it out of the house of Abinadab which was at Gibeah, accompanying the ark of God: and Ahio went before the ark.

And David and all the house of Israel played before the Lord on all manner of instruments made of fir wood, even on harps, and on psalteries, and on timbrels, and on cornets, and on cymbals.

And when they came to Nachon's threshingfloor, Uzzah put forth his hand to the ark of God, and took hold of it; for the oxen shook it.

And the anger of the Lord was kindled against Uzzah; and God smote him there for his error; and there he died by the ark of God.

And David was displeased, because the Lord had made a breach upon Uzzah: and he called the name of the place Perezuzzah to this day.

And David was afraid of the Lord that day, and said, How shall the ark of the Lord come to me?

So David would not remove the ark of the Lord unto him into the city of David: but David carried it aside into the house of Obededom the Gittite.

And the ark of the Lord continued in the house of Obededom the Gittite three months: and the Lord blessed Obededom, and all his household.

And it was told king David, saying, The Lord hath blessed the house of Obededom, and all that pertaineth unto him, because of the ark of God. So David went and brought up the ark of God from the house of Obededom into the city of David with gladness.

And it was so, that when they that bare the ark of the Lord had gone six paces, he sacrificed oxen and fatlings.

And David danced before the Lord with all his might; and David was girded with a linen ephod.

So David and all the house of Israel brought up the ark of the Lord with shouting, and with the sound of the trumpet.

Hebrews 12:1:

Wherefore, seeing we also are compassed about with so great a cloud of witnesses, let us lay aside every weight, and the sin which doth so easily beset us, and let us run with patience the race that is set before us.

Chapter Three
God Wants You to Live In Victory

"Nay, in all these things we are more
than conquerors through him that loved us."

Romans 8:37

Genesis 1:3-4:

> And God said, Let there be light: and there was light.
>
> And God saw the light, that it was good: and God divided the light from the darkness.

Matthew 8:12:

> But the children of the kingdom shall be cast out into outer darkness: there shall be weeping and gnashing of teeth.

1 Corinthians 3:1-3:

> And I, brethren, could not speak unto you as unto spiritual, but as unto carnal, even as unto babes in Christ.
>
> I have fed you with milk, and not with meat: for hitherto ye were not able to bear it, neither yet now are ye able.
>
> For ye are yet carnal: for whereas there is among you envying, and strife, and divisions, are ye not carnal, and walk as men?

Luke 10:23:

> And he turned him unto his disciples, and said privately, Blessed are the eyes which see the things that ye see.

Matthew 8:11:

> And I say unto you, That many shall come from the east and west, and shall sit down with Abraham, and Isaac, and Jacob, in the kingdom of heaven.

Proverbs 15:1:

> A soft answer turneth away wrath: but grievous words stir up anger.

Exodus 32:1-4:

> And when the people saw that Moses delayed to come down out of the mount, the people gathered themselves together unto Aaron, and said unto him, Up, make us gods, which shall go before us; for as for this Moses, the man that brought us up out of the land of Egypt, we wot not what is become of him.
>
> And Aaron said unto them, Break off the golden earrings, which are in the ears of your wives, of your sons, and of your daughters, and bring them unto me.

And all the people brake off the golden earrings which were in their ears, and brought them unto Aaron.

And he received them at their hand, and fashioned it with a graving tool, after he had made it a molten calf: and they said, These be thy gods, O Israel, which brought thee up out of the land of Egypt.

Exodus 32:6:

And they rose up early on the morrow, and offered burnt offerings, and brought peace offerings; and the people sat down to eat and to drink, and rose up to play.

Exodus 32:14:

And the Lord repented of the evil which he thought to do unto his people.

Psalm 136: 2-4:

O give thanks unto the God of gods: for his mercy endureth for ever.

O give thanks to the Lord of lords: for his mercy endureth for ever.

To him who alone doeth great wonders: for his mercy endureth for ever.

Matthew 8:13:

> And Jesus said unto the centurion, Go thy way; and as thou hast believed, so be it done unto thee. And his servant was healed in the selfsame hour.

John 14:12:

> Verily, verily, I say unto you, He that believeth on me, the works that I do shall he do also; and greater works than these shall he do; because I go unto my Father.

Part II — Who Am I Really?

Chapter Four

Understand You Are a Child of God

> *"Beloved, now are we the sons of God, and it doth not yet appear what we shall be: but we know that, when he shall appear, we shall be like him; for we shall see him as he is."*
>
> **1 John 3:2**

Ephesians 1:5:

> Having predestinated us unto the adoption of children by Jesus Christ to himself, according to the good pleasure of his will.

Matthew 25:19-29:

After a long time the lord of those servants cometh, and reckoneth with them.

And so he that had received five talents came and brought other five talents, saying, Lord, thou deliveredst unto me five talents: behold, I have gained beside them five talents more.

His lord said unto him, Well done, thou good and faithful servant: thou hast been faithful over a few things, I will make thee ruler over many things: enter thou into the joy of thy lord.

He also that had received two talents came and said, Lord, thou deliveredst unto me two talents: behold, I have gained two other talents beside them.

His lord said unto him, Well done, good and faithful servant; thou hast been faithful over a few things, I will make thee ruler over many things: enter thou into the joy of thy lord.

Then he which had received the one talent came and said, Lord, I knew thee that thou art a hard man, reaping where thou hast not sown, and gathering where thou hast not strewed:

And I was afraid, and went and hid thy talent in the earth: lo, there thou hast that is thine.

His lord answered and said unto him, Thou wicked and slothful servant, thou knewest that I reap where I sowed not, and gather where I have not strewed:

Thou oughtest therefore to have put my money to the exchangers, and then at my coming I should have received mine own with usury.

Take therefore the talent from him, and give it unto him which hath ten talents.

For unto every one that hath shall be given, and he shall have abundance: but from him that hath not shall be taken away even that which he hath.

Hebrews 12:1:

Wherefore, seeing we also are compassed about with so great a cloud of witnesses, let us lay aside every weight, and the sin which doth so easily beset us, and let us run with patience the race that is set before us.

Mark 4:3-13:

Hearken; Behold, there went out a sower to sow:

And it came to pass, as he sowed, some fell by the wayside, and the fowls of the air came and devoured it up.

And some fell on stony ground, where it had not much earth; and immediately it sprang up, because it had no depth of earth:

But when the sun was up, it was scorched; and because it had no root, it withered away.

And some fell among thorns, and the thorns grew up, and choked it, and it yielded no fruit.

And other fell on good ground, and did yield fruit that sprang up and increased; and brought forth, some thirty, and some sixty, and some a hundred.

And he said unto them, He that hath ears to hear, let him hear.

And when he was alone, they that were about him with the twelve asked of him the parable.

And he said unto them, Unto you it is given to know the mystery of the kingdom of God: but unto them that are without, all these things are done in parables:

That seeing they may see, and not perceive; and hearing they may hear, and not understand; lest at any time they should be converted, and their sins should be forgiven them.

And he said unto them, Know ye not this parable? and how then will ye know all parables?

Mark 4:35-40:

> And the same day, when the even was come, he saith unto them, Let us pass over unto the other side.

> And when they had sent away the multitude, they took him even as he was in the ship. And there were also with him other little ships.

> And there arose a great storm of wind, and the waves beat into the ship, so that it was now full.

> And he was in the hinder part of the ship, asleep on a pillow: and they awake him, and say unto him, Master, carest thou not that we perish?

> And he arose, and rebuked the wind, and said unto the sea, Peace, be still. And the wind ceased, and there was a great calm.

> And he said unto them, Why are ye so fearful? how is it that ye have no faith?

Galatians 2:20:

> I am crucified with Christ: nevertheless I live; yet not I, but Christ liveth in me: and the life which I now live in the flesh I live by the faith of the Son of God, who loved me, and gave himself for me.

Luke 2:40,52:

> And the child grew, and waxed strong in spirit, filled with wisdom: and the grace of God was upon him.

> And Jesus increased in wisdom and stature, and in favor with God and man.

Chapter Five
God Inspires and Initiates

> *"The hand of the Lord was upon me . . ."*
>
> **Ezekiel 37:1**

Genesis 15:2-5:

> And Abram said, Lord God, what wilt thou give me, seeing I go childless, and the steward of my house is this Eliezer of Damascus?

> And Abram said, Behold, to me thou hast given no seed: and, lo, one born in my house is mine heir.

> And, behold, the word of the Lord came unto him, saying, This shall not be thine heir; but he that shall come forth out of thine own bowels shall be thine heir.

> And he brought him forth abroad, and said, Look now toward heaven, and tell the stars, if thou be able to number them: and he said unto him, So shall thy seed be.

Genesis 16:1-16:

Now Sarai Abram's wife bare him no children: and she had a handmaid, an Egyptian, whose name was Hagar.

And Sarai said unto Abram, Behold now, the Lord hath restrained me from bearing: I pray thee, go in unto my maid; it may be that I may obtain children by her. And Abram hearkened to the voice of Sarai.

And Sarai, Abram's wife, took Hagar her maid the Egyptian, after Abram had dwelt ten years in the land of Canaan, and gave her to her husband Abram to be his wife.

And he went in unto Hagar, and she conceived: and when she saw that she had conceived, her mistress was despised in her eyes.

And Sarai said unto Abram, My wrong be upon thee: I have given my maid into thy bosom; and when she saw that she had conceived, I was despised in her eyes: the Lord judge between me and thee.

But Abram said unto Sarai, Behold, thy maid is in thine hand; do to her as it pleaseth thee. And when Sarai dealt hardly with her, she fled from her face.

And the angel of the Lord found her by a fountain of water in the wilderness, by the fountain in the way to Shur.

And he said, Hagar, Sarai's maid, whence camest thou? and whither wilt thou go? And she said, I flee from the face of my mistress Sarai.

And the angel of the Lord said unto her, Return to thy mistress, and submit thyself under her hands.

And the angel of the Lord said unto her, I will multiply thy seed exceedingly, that it shall not be numbered for multitude.

And the angel of the Lord said unto her, Behold, thou art with child and shalt bear a son, and shalt call his name Ishmael; because the Lord hath heard thy affliction.

And he will be a wild man; his hand will be against every man, and every man's hand against him; and he shall dwell in the presence of all his brethren.

And she called the name of the Lord that spake unto her, Thou God seest me: for she said, Have I also here looked after him that seeth me?

Wherefore the well was called Beerlahairoi; behold, it is between Kadesh and Bered.

And Hagar bare Abram a son: and Abram called his son's name, which Hagar bare, Ishmael.

And Abram was fourscore and six years old, when Hagar bare Ishmael to Abram.

Genesis 21:1-3

> And the Lord visited Sarah as he had said, and the Lord did unto Sarah as he had spoken.

> For Sarah conceived, and bare Abraham a son in his old age, at the set time of which God had spoken to him.

> And Abraham called the name of his son that was born unto him, whom Sarah bare to him, Isaac.

Proverbs 15:31:

> The ear that heareth the reproof of life abideth among the wise.

1 Corinthians 11:28:

> But let a man examine himself, and so let him eat of that bread, and drink of that cup.

James 1:2-4:

> My brethren, count it all joy when ye fall into divers temptations;

> Knowing this, that the trying of your faith worketh patience.

> But let patience have her perfect work, that ye may be perfect and entire, wanting nothing.

Part III — What Do I Choose?

Chapter Six
Growing Up and Maturing is a Personal Choice

"When I was a child, I spake as a child,
I understood as a child, I thought as a child:
but when I became a man, I put away childish things."
1 Corinthians 13:11

Matthew 3:16-17:

> And Jesus, when he was baptized, went up straightway out of the water: and, lo, the heavens were opened unto him, and he saw the Spirit of God descending like a dove, and lighting upon him:
>
> And lo a voice from heaven, saying, This is my beloved Son, in whom I am well pleased.

Matthew 4:17:

> From that time Jesus began to preach, and to say, Repent: for the kingdom of heaven is at hand.

Amos 5:24:

> But let judgment run down as waters, and righteousness as a mighty stream.

Job 1:12-21:

And the Lord said unto Satan, Behold, all that he hath is in thy power; only upon himself put not forth thine hand. So Satan went forth from the presence of the Lord.

And there was a day when his sons and his daughters were eating and drinking wine in their eldest brother's house:

And there came a messenger unto Job, and said, The oxen were plowing, and the asses feeding beside them:

And the Sabeans fell upon them, and took them away; yea, they have slain the servants with the edge of the sword; and I only am escaped alone to tell thee.

While he was yet speaking, there came also another, and said, The fire of God is fallen from heaven, and hath burned up the sheep, and the servants, and consumed them; and I only am escaped alone to tell thee.

While he was yet speaking, there came also another, and said, The Chaldeans made out three bands, and fell upon the camels, and have carried them away, yea, and slain the servants with the edge of the sword; and I only am escaped alone to tell thee.

While he was yet speaking, there came also another, and said, Thy sons and thy daughters were eating and drinking wine in their eldest brother's house:

And, behold, there came a great wind from the wilderness,

and smote the four corners of the house, and it fell upon the young men, and they are dead; and I only am escaped alone to tell thee.

Then Job arose, and rent his mantle, and shaved his head, and fell down upon the ground, and worshipped,

And said, Naked came I out of my mother's womb, and naked shall I return thither: the Lord gave, and the Lord hath taken away; blessed be the name of the Lord.

Job 2:6-7:

And the Lord said unto Satan, Behold, he is in thine hand; but save his life.

So went Satan forth from the presence of the Lord, and smote Job with sore boils from the sole of his foot unto his crown.

Genesis 1:28:

And God blessed them, and God said unto them, Be fruitful, and multiply, and replenish the earth, and subdue it: and have dominion over the fish of the sea, and over the fowl of the air, and over every living thing that moveth upon the earth.

Luke 15:11-32:

And he said, A certain man had two sons:

And the younger of them said to his father, Father, give me the portion of goods that falleth to me. And he divided unto them his living.

And not many days after the younger son gathered all together, and took his journey into a far country, and there wasted his substance with riotous living.

And when he had spent all, there arose a mighty famine in that land; and he began to be in want.

And he went and joined himself to a citizen of that country; and he sent him into his fields to feed swine.

And he would fain have filled his belly with the husks that the swine did eat: and no man gave unto him.

And when he came to himself, he said, How many hired servants of my father's have bread enough and to spare, and I perish with hunger!

I will arise and go to my father, and will say unto him, Father, I have sinned against heaven, and before thee,

And am no more worthy to be called thy son: make me as one of thy hired servants.

And he arose, and came to his father. But when he was yet a great way off, his father saw him, and had compassion, and ran, and fell on his neck, and kissed him.

And the son said unto him, Father, I have sinned against heaven, and in thy sight, and am no more worthy to be called thy son.

But the father said to his servants, Bring forth the best robe, and put it on him; and put a ring on his hand, and shoes on his feet:

And bring hither the fatted calf, and kill it; and let us eat, and be merry:

For this my son was dead, and is alive again; he was lost, and is found. And they began to be merry.

Now his elder son was in the field: and as he came and drew nigh to the house, he heard music and dancing.

And he called one of the servants, and asked what these things meant.

And he said unto him, Thy brother is come; and thy father hath killed the fatted calf, because he hath received him safe and sound.

And he was angry, and would not go in: therefore came his father out, and entreated him.

And he answering said to his father, Lo, these many years do I serve thee, neither transgressed I at any time thy commandment; and yet thou never gavest me a kid, that I might make merry with my friends:

But as soon as this thy son was come, which hath devoured thy living with harlots, thou hast killed for him the fatted calf.

And he said unto him, Son, thou art ever with me, and all that I have is thine.

It was meet that we should make merry, and be glad: for this thy brother was dead, and is alive again; and was lost, and is found.

Matthew 7:11:

If ye then, being evil, know how to give good gifts unto your children, how much more shall your Father which is in heaven give good things to them that ask him?

Mark 10:38:

But Jesus said unto them, Ye know not what ye ask: can ye drink of the cup that I drink of? and be baptized with the baptism that I am baptized with?

Acts 8:5-24:

Then Philip went down to the city of Samaria, and preached Christ unto them.

And the people with one accord gave heed unto those things which Philip spake, hearing and seeing the miracles which he did.

For unclean spirits, crying with loud voice, came out of many that were possessed with them: and many taken with palsies, and that were lame, were healed.

And there was great joy in that city.

But there was a certain man, called Simon, which beforetime in the same city used sorcery, and bewitched the people of Samaria, giving out that himself was some great one:

To whom they all gave heed, from the least to the greatest, saying, This man is the great power of God.

And to him they had regard, because that of long time he had bewitched them with sorceries.

But when they believed Philip preaching the things concerning the kingdom of God, and the name of Jesus Christ, they were baptized, both men and women.

Then Simon himself believed also: and when he was baptized, he continued with Philip, and wondered, beholding the miracles and signs which were done.

Now when the apostles which were at Jerusalem heard that Samaria had received the word of God, they sent unto them Peter and John:

Who, when they were come down, prayed for them, that they might receive the Holy Ghost:

(For as yet he was fallen upon none of them: only they were baptized in the name of the Lord Jesus.)

Then laid they their hands on them, and they received the Holy Ghost.

And when Simon saw that through laying on of the apostles' hands the Holy Ghost was given, he offered them money,

Saying, Give me also this power, that on whomsoever I lay hands, he may receive the Holy Ghost.

But Peter said unto him, Thy money perish with thee, because thou hast thought that the gift of God may be purchased with money.

Thou hast neither part nor lot in this matter: for thy heart is not right in the sight of God.

Repent therefore of this thy wickedness, and pray God, if perhaps the thought of thine heart may be forgiven thee.

For I perceive that thou art in the gall of bitterness, and in the bond of iniquity.

Then answered Simon, and said, Pray ye to the Lord for me, that none of these things which ye have spoken come upon me.

Chapter Seven

Select Friends Wisely

"Make no friendship with an angry man;
and with a furious man thou shalt not go."

Proverbs 22:24

Proverbs 18:24:

> A man that hath friends must show himself friendly: and there is a friend that sticketh closer than a brother.

Hebrews 5:13-14:

> For every one that useth milk is unskilful in the word of righteousness: for he is a babe.
>
> But strong meat belongeth to them that are of full age, even those who by reason of use have their senses exercised to discern both good and evil.

John 14:26:

> But the Comforter, which is the Holy Ghost, whom the Father will send in my name, he shall teach you all things, and bring all things to your remembrance, whatsoever I have said unto you.

Genesis 3:14:

> And the Lord God said unto the serpent, Because thou hast done this, thou art cursed above all cattle, and above every beast of the field; upon thy belly shalt thou go, and dust shalt thou eat all the days of thy life.

Matthew 28:19-20:

> Go ye therefore, and teach all nations, baptizing them in the name of the Father, and of the Son, and of the Holy Ghost:

> Teaching them to observe all things whatsoever I have commanded you: and, lo, I am with you alway, even unto the end of the world. Amen.

Part IV — What Is My Purpose?

Chapter Eight
Know That You Are Given Authority

> *"And God said, Let us make man in our image, after our likeness: and let them have dominion over the fish of the sea, and over the fowl of the air, and over the cattle, and over all the earth, and over every creeping thing that creepeth upon the earth."*
>
> **Genesis 1:26**

Matthew 6:10:

> Thy kingdom come. Thy will be done in earth, as it is in heaven.

Acts 3:6:

> Then Peter said, Silver and gold have I none; but such as I have give I thee: In the name of Jesus Christ of Nazareth rise up and walk.

Acts 3:7-8:

> And he took him by the right hand, and lifted him up: and immediately his feet and ankle bones received strength.

> And he leaping up stood, and walked, and entered with them into the temple, walking, and leaping, and praising God.

John 20:22:

> And when he had said this, he breathed on them, and saith unto them, Receive ye the Holy Ghost.

Romans 8:19:

> For the earnest expectation of the creature waiteth for the manifestation of the sons of God.

John 17:15:

> I pray not that thou shouldest take them out of the world, but that thou shouldest keep them from the evil.

Matthew 16:16:

> And Simon Peter answered and said, Thou art the Christ, the Son of the living God.

Daniel 2:44-45:

> And in the days of these kings shall the God of heaven set up a kingdom, which shall never be destroyed: and the kingdom shall not be left to other people, but it shall break in pieces and consume all these kingdoms, and it shall stand for ever.

> Forasmuch as thou sawest that the stone was cut out of the mountain without hands, and that it brake in pieces the iron, the brass, the clay, the silver, and the gold; the great God hath made known to the king what shall come to pass hereafter: and the dream is certain, and the interpretation thereof sure.

Chapter Nine
Change Happens

"And it shall come to pass, if thou shalt hearken diligently unto the voice of the Lord thy God, to observe and to do all his commandments which I command thee this day, that the Lord thy God will set thee on high above all nations of the earth."

Deuteronomy 28:1

Ecclesiastes 3:1:

> To every thing there is a season, and a time to every purpose under the heaven.

Ecclesiastes 3:9-10:

> What profit hath he that worketh in that wherein he laboureth?
>
> I have seen the travail, which God hath given to the sons of men to be exercised in it.

Luke 1:26-38:

> And in the sixth month the angel Gabriel was sent from God unto a city of Galilee, named Nazareth,
>
> To a virgin espoused to a man whose name was Joseph, of the house of David; and the virgin's name was Mary.

And the angel came in unto her, and said, Hail, thou that art highly favoured, the Lord is with thee: blessed art thou among women.

And when she saw him, she was troubled at his saying, and cast in her mind what manner of salutation this should be.

And the angel said unto her, Fear not, Mary: for thou hast found favour with God.

And, behold, thou shalt conceive in thy womb, and bring forth a son, and shalt call his name Jesus.

He shall be great, and shall be called the Son of the Highest: and the Lord God shall give unto him the throne of his father David:

And he shall reign over the house of Jacob for ever; and of his kingdom there shall be no end.

Then said Mary unto the angel, How shall this be, seeing I know not a man?

And the angel answered and said unto her, The Holy Ghost shall come upon thee, and the power of the Highest shall overshadow thee: therefore also that holy thing which shall be born of thee shall be called the Son of God.

And, behold, thy cousin Elisabeth, she hath also conceived a son in her old age: and this is the sixth month with her, who was called barren.

For with God nothing shall be impossible.

And Mary said, Behold the handmaid of the Lord; be it unto me according to thy word. And the angel departed from her.

Chapter Ten
Know the Purpose of God's Anointing Upon Your Life

"But the anointing which ye have received of him abideth in you, and ye need not that any man teach you: but as the same anointing teacheth you of all things, and is truth, and is no lie, and even as it hath taught you, ye shall abide in him."
1 John 2:27

Mark 4:12:

That seeing they may see, and not perceive; and hearing they may hear, and not understand; lest at any time they should be converted, and their sins should be forgiven them.

Psalm 63:6:

When I remember thee upon my bed, and meditate on thee in the night watches.

Colossians 1:26-27:

Even the mystery which hath been hid from ages and from generations, but now is made manifest to his saints:

To whom God would make known what is the riches of the glory of this mystery among the Gentiles; which is Christ in you, the hope of glory.

ABOUT THE AUTHOR

Kevin West is the executive pastor of Christ Temple Church in Huntington, West Virginia and the president of KW Ministries. He broadcasts daily on his radio program, *Real Life with Pastor Kevin West*. Kevin and his wife, Leesa, have four children and one grandchild.

J.F. Edwards is an award-winning author who has also taught writing for twenty-six years. He holds an M.F.A. in Creative Writing (Bowling Green State University) and an M.A. in English (Marshall University).

Need additional copies?

To order more copies of

LIVING A TRANSFORMED LIFE

contact NewBookPublishing.com

❏ Order online at:

NewBookPublishing.com/Bookstore

❏ Call 877-311-5100 or

❏ Email Info@NewBookPublishing.com

Call for multiple copy discounts!

Reliance Media